Caring for
Ourselves

A Therapist's Guide to Personal
and Professional Well-Being

Caring for Ourselves

A Therapist's Guide to Personal and Professional Well-Being

Ellen K. Baker

American Psychological Association • *Washington, DC*

Published by
American Psychological Association
750 First Street, NE
Washington, DC 20002
www.apa.org

To order
APA Order Department
P.O. Box 92984
Washington, DC 20090-2984
Tel: (800) 374-2721, Direct: (202) 336-5510
Fax: (202) 336-5502, TDD/TTY: (202) 336-6123
Online: www.apa.org/books/
E-mail: order@apa.org

In the U.K., Europe, Africa, and the Middle East, copies may be ordered from
American Psychological Association
3 Henrietta Street
Covent Garden, London
WC2E 8LU England

Typeset in Meridien by EPS Group Inc., Easton, MD

Printer: United Book Press, Baltimore, MD
Cover Designer: Naylor Design, Washington, DC
Technical/Production Editor: Jen Powers

The opinions and statements published are the responsibility of the authors, and such opinions and statements do not necessarily represent the policies of the American Psychological Association.

Library of Congress Cataloging-in-Publication Data
Baker, Ellen K.
   Taking care of ourselves : a therapist's guide to personal and professional well-being / Ellen K. Baker.
      p. cm
Includes bibliographical references and index.
   ISBN 1-55798-934-6
   1. Psychotherapists—Health and hygiene.   2. Psychotherapists—Conduct of life.   I. Title.
   RC480.5 .B275 2002
   616.89′14′023—dc21

                                                                        2002002413

British Library Cataloguing-in-Publication Data
A CIP record is available from the British Library.

Printed in the United States of America
First Edition

Contents

6

Preface

As therapists, we use our training and skills to help our patients become more self-aware and more self-tending. Many of us, however, are reluctant for a gamut of reasons to offer ourselves that same kind of understanding and care. Yet in reality, self-care, personally and professionally, may ultimately be the most important thing that we do—not just for ourselves but also for our clients.

Each of us brings our own personal and professional history to the practice of self-care. This history can both help and complicate that process.

I was born the first of five children to parents who grew up during the Great Depression and World War II. When I was a child, my father was a country veterinarian, with a large- and small-animal practice in a small town in the Midwest. The pace of life in our home, and in most homes following the war, was fast and intense. My father was on 24-hour call. I remember being told that a cow didn't know what time of day it was when she had trouble calving. My mother was my father's unofficial assistant. She was devoted to him and to the practice. In another age, she would have been a veterinarian herself.

Now retired from private practice, my father continues to participate in his local, state, and national professional associations. Eighty-three years old at the time of this writing, he drives 100 miles each way weekly to sit on the admissions board of a major state university vet school.

I saw and absorbed a model of being involved and giving: to clients—those who could pay, and those who couldn't; to family —a large and extended one, including a later-born sibling with a developmental disability; and to community—a small town and rural setting where people knew each other and many were related.

The values I took in—of ambition, hard work, friendship, and compassion—have served me well. I have reaped many benefits by being acculturated to attune to others' needs and to be an active part of a larger whole, among them the pleasure of adopting psychology and psychotherapy as a vocation. It has been a good fit for me. Being emotionally present with another person's humanness is both deeply gratifying and humbling.

Like all other human beings, I have had my own challenges and struggles at various stages of my personal and professional development. As a young professional, it became dramatically apparent that I needed to better understand and tend to my own feelings. I became conscious that it was not only all right, but essential, to take charge of my own life. To observe and replenish, to be respectful of my needs, and to practice regulation in the service of those needs became indispensable tasks. As a mature practitioner, I continue to be acutely aware of the need to balance attention to self and others—to tend to my own physical, psychological, and spiritual needs and to balance my personal and professional selves. Responsible self-care is a complex trial-and-error process that lasts a lifetime.

My lifelong involvement in the expressive arts of music, drama, and dance has allowed me to gain access to and express inchoate emotions seemingly yearning to be owned and integrated. Several years back, as a gift to myself on turning 50, I committed weekly time for dance class, something that previously had gotten lost in the tasks and demands of earlier life stages. My life, personally and thereby professionally, has been enriched in the process. I hope that this book will lead you to similar sources of enrichment.

Several years ago, as part of my journey in the self-care process, I led an experiential workshop titled "Respecting and Nourishing Ourselves as Therapists: A Psychodramatic Exploration." The participants in that session were immensely responsive; they seemed hungry for further consideration of the topic. That session subsequently led to a series of experiential workshops, presented at American Psychological Association conventions and other conferences, on therapist self-care conceptualized in terms of personal and professional awareness and regulation. It was in these workshop settings, and through informal talks with colleagues, that I grasped the intensity and depth of my own interest and satisfaction in facilitating, sharing, and exploring the self-care process with other clinicians. This book is an outgrowth of this ongoing involvement and commitment. Upon undertaking the writing of this book, I interviewed a select, nonrandom sample of nearly 30 practitioners diverse in age, stage of career, gender, ethnicity, sexual orientation, and form of employment (self or salaried). The resulting discussions were rich in perspective. Some of that material is shared in this book.

In the early stages of this book, one of the interviewees, Michael Mahoney, who gave generously of his time and his reflections, suggested that such undertakings often have personal, as well as professional, influence on one's life. I wondered at the time if his remark would hold true for me. To my amazement, in the course of writing this book, I have, in fact, had the experience of becoming more accepting of my self—my needs, my vulnerabilities, my yearnings, and my limits. I have grown in my capacity to stay present and to care for myself in my own humanness. I am deeply grateful for the opportunity to write this book and for the support I have received from my fellow therapists in this process.

Caring for Ourselves

A Therapist's Guide to Personal
and Professional Well-Being

Introduction

For most of us, working as a psychotherapist brings many rewards, from intellectual, emotional, and spiritual challenges to opportunities for personal growth, status, and material success. Nonetheless, our work can also be intensely demanding, frustrating at moments, and sometimes terrifying.

As therapists we share the same pain and joys of human existence as our patients. Most of us, when we're honest or pressed, feel very human indeed. We may rationally believe in the value of responsible self-care. Many of us are truly masterful in helping others learn about and practice self-care. Yet many of us struggle with conflicts and deterrents to our own self-care.

Self-care as a healthy and valuable process is being widely discussed these days. A number of books on the general trade market address the benefits of self-care, self-nurturance (Domar, 2000), self-nourishment (McKay, Beck, & Sutker, 2001), and related topics. Certainly, self-care is a responsible practice—for all human beings—and indisputably for those employed in the service and care of others.

This book focuses on self-care for therapists as a group of caregivers with particular concerns and needs. It begins by examining conceptual issues (the domains, dynamics, and conflicts associated with therapist self-care) and moves on to suggest ways that we, as therapists, can attain or maintain balance in our personal and professional lives. A range of theoretical, professional, and personal sources are cited throughout the book. These citations serve to direct you to further reading if you so desire and to give due credit to those who have contributed to the sense of community and critical mass of voices emerging with respect to the imperative for therapist self-care.

Audience

This book is addressed to psychologists who work as psychotherapists, whatever their stage of personal and professional development or clinical orientation. Self-care is a lifespan issue, personally and professionally, whatever our theoretical or clinical worldview. Although this book was written from the perspective of a psychologist in private practice, much of the material is relevant to psychologists who work in schools, university counseling centers, managed care organizations, community mental health centers, and business or industry settings. Likewise, other mental health professionals, including psychiatrists, social workers, and marriage and family counselors, will likely find relevant the discussion of self-care in this book.

For younger, less-experienced clinicians, the book can be an orientation to the topic of therapist self-care. The book is written as a version of what I would have benefited from as a young psychology trainee. It is appropriate for graduate and continuing education course work on ethics and professional issues in clinical and counseling psychology or on psychotherapy theory, research, and practice; it also constitutes resource material for psychotherapy practice. For more seasoned therapists, this book provides a resource for addressing, and readdressing, an issue that can be elusive and conflictual, whatever our age or level of experience.

Objectives of This Book

This book presents self-awareness and self-regulation as a means to balance connection with self, with others, and with the universe across the personal and professional lifespan of the therapist. This book offers information, support, reassurance, and validation toward this goal.

The objectives of the book are as follows:

1. to stimulate and enable therapists, of all ages and stages, to develop and institute a conscious, ongoing practice of personal and professional self-care;
2. to advocate the need and value of normalizing therapist self-care;
3. to foster communication among therapists on the subject of self-care to help them confront loneliness and isolation of work in the field;

4. to organize and share information, resources, and various perspectives on the process of therapist self-care and thus to contribute to the evolving therapist self-care literature; and
5. to support ongoing education and research pertinent to therapist self-care.

Language

For the purposes of the book, I have made several choices regarding terminology. I use the first-person plural (that is, *we, us,* and *our*) because I share with many other therapists the issues discussed in this book. Although unwieldy, the occasional use of *he or she* or *him or her* reflects the fact that the need for self-care applies to all therapists, regardless of gender.

I use the terms *patient* and *client* interchangeably, with the understanding that the former has a medical connotation for some and the latter a commercial connotation for others. *Psychologist, clinician, therapist, psychotherapist, practitioner,* and *health care professional* are also used interchangeably, although I recognize that the terms have varying connotations.

Theoretical Framework

The book is written from the perspective of a biopsychosocial model of human behavior. Contemporary research provides evidence that people's lives are affected by ongoing interactions among their genetic and biological, psychological, and environmental influences (Wachs, 2000). Neuroscientific research continues to further illuminate an interactive bidirectional mind–body relationship—between physical functioning and emotional responses, between psychological experience and physiological manifestations (Baum & Posluszny, 1999; Kiecolt-Glaser, 1999). We all possess inherited capacities and vulnerabilities based on our genetic makeup, but environmental influences may maximize or minimize that inheritance. For example, our DNA may leave us susceptible to certain diseases, but how we live everyday life and the effects of traumatic experience, can significantly impact physiological functioning, influencing our ability to prevent and control those diseases (Ratey, 1998; van der Kolk, McFarlane, & Weisaeth, 1996; Vaughan, 1998).

A subject as broad and comprehensive as that of therapist self-care benefits from a broad-based theoretical orientation that considers character development as well as symptom reduction and coping strategies (Frank, 1977). Lifespan development, self psychology, object relations, and relational theories all are used in examining the stages and process of self-care.

Lifespan development theory offers therapists a perspective for considering our own developmental stages and changes across the lifespan, personally and professionally. Each life stage has its corresponding benefits, opportunities, goals, challenges, risks, conflicts, and crises, both personally and professionally, that bear examination (Coster & Schwebel, 1997; Goldberg, 1991; Guy, 1987; Lindner, 1990). This book will help readers consider the sequences and patterns of change they have experienced and reflect on individual differences and the multidirectionality of change with age (Lachman & James, 1997).

The significance of relationship—with self, as well as with others—is core to self-care. This book draws on self psychology and object relations theory to help readers focus on within- and between-self relations. Self psychology theory speaks to the importance of the structure and cohesion, as well as the development, of the self. Object relations theory provides a means of thinking about our relationships with self and with others (Mahler, 1968). Winnicott's (1965) notions of the "true self" and "good-enough" functioning are immensely valuable to the discussion and practice of therapist self-care. Relational theory holds that interpersonal connectedness is essential for emotional health (J. B. Miller, Jordan, Kaplan, Stiver, & Surrey, 1991) and reminds us that therapists, as well as patients, are affected by the experience of the relationship.

Therapist Interviews

Throughout the book, excerpts drawn from interviews done with a select, nonrandom sample of more than 30 practitioners are shared. The interviewees represent a diverse group of psychologists in terms of clinical orientation, age, career stage (active and retired), gender, race, geography, sexual orientation, and form of employment (self or salaried). A number of the interviewees are psychologists who have published in the area of therapist self-care. Interviews were audiotaped in person or over the telephone and ranged from under an hour to 3 hours. Confidentiality was assured, as was the right to approve quoted material.

Interview questions were divided into 3 categories: professional self, therapist self-experience (in terms of emotional demands and stresses and self-care), and related questions. The questions were derived from a number of sources, including Cantor and Bernay, 1992; Goldberg, 1992; Guy, 1987; Mahoney, 1997; Saakvitne & Pearlman, 1996; Sussman, 1992; and my own work. This interview questionnaire is offered to readers on pages 55–58.

Although not within the scope of this book, an in-depth analysis and discussion of the therapist interview material would be extremely interesting and valuable in its own right. The participating therapists, individually and collectively, spoke thoughtfully and generously.

Format

The format of this book is similar to that of an experiential workshop designed to explore and develop therapist self-care awareness and skills.[1] You are invited to use this book as an experimental guide for the self-care process.

Chapters 1 and 2 introduce the concept of self-care and the rationale for practicing it. They represent the "why" of therapist self-care as a prelude to the more interactive "how" of care, which is attaining balance and connection. Chapter 1 operationalizes the concept of self-care as comprising self-awareness, self-regulation, and balance. It describes therapist stress and reports on the state of the research on therapist distress, burnout, and impairment. Chapter 2 describes developmental issues in therapist self-care.

Chapters 3 through 6 parallel the action segment of an experiential workshop. Here, you are invited to interact with the material by using the various topics discussed as a springboard for journaling about your own observations and reactions. Chapter 3 examines the nature of the self and the forces that shape it. Readers may find it worthwhile to complete the therapist self-care self-

---

[1] *Experiential* refers to techniques and process, grounded in psychological theory, designed to facilitate "awareness of feelings, perceptions, cognitions, and sensations; that is . . . in-the-moment experience. The method usually involves some degree of action . . . either physical or imagined" (Hornyak & Baker, 1989, p. 3). An experiential workshop is organized in three parts: (a) "introduction" to the material, (b) "action" section with experiential exercises, and (c) "closing" or sharing about the content and process of the workshop.

assessment questionnaire in the appendix to chapter 3 as a means of assessing self-awareness of self-care issues, achievements, and deficits. Chapter 4 delves further into the psychological, physical, and spiritual aspects of self that require care. Chapter 5 addresses self-care of our professional self, and chapter 6 discusses how to care for self in our relationships with others. These categories, although used as an organizing structure, are, of course, somewhat arbitrary. In reality, our mind and body, our self and others, and our personal and professional selves interact in infinitely complex ways.

The Epilogue parallels the closing of an experiential workshop session; it provides recommendations for graduate and postgraduate education and discusses professional and associational involvement in therapist self-care. The Epilogue also includes a final set of journal writing questions to spur you to reflect on the content and process of your experience of reading and writing about self-care.

Personal Journal Writing

The most important experiential action component of this book is personal journal writing. As in an experiential workshop, readers are invited, at various points in each chapter, to reflect on their "in the moment" intellectual and emotional responses to the material covered. Other thoughts and feelings directly or indirectly related to self-care may also come forth in the writing process. As we often say in therapy, "Trust the process." Material that comes to mind is coming from somewhere within and likely has meaning, whether or not that is immediately apparent.

Personal journal writing is defined here as a collection of dated entries accumulated over time containing notations on feelings, experiences, and dreams. Quotations, fantasies, sketches, or other matters may also be included. Journal writing can help process feelings and deepen self-awareness. It can assist in the service of self-regulation and self-management; contain, diffuse, and metabolize tension; and facilitate coping with emotional upheaval and trauma (Smyth & Pennebaker, 1999).

Journal writing also offers us a means for developing a deeper relationship with our self. It provides a place and means for "being with the self" in the "here and now," in the Kohutian self psychological sense of self-mirroring and self-soothing:

It has come to be very comforting to know that I can make notes to myself, over the course of my day, of various thoughts and feelings, from which I can later expand upon in my journal. Likewise, there are moments of pride, pleasure, satisfaction, and/or intrigue with feelings or thoughts that I look forward to later being with in the journal. The journal seems to help me stay connected with, as well as deal with, my humanness. It continues to be immensely gratifying to me to discover that I can tolerate, and even move further towards making peace with parts of the self that, at times, have felt threatening. In keeping a journal, the implicit message to the self is that our feelings are real, tolerable, and worthy of our care and attention. (Baker, 1990, p. 34)

PROCESS OF JOURNAL WRITING

Because journal writing is a very personal activity, a wide variety of approaches exist. Individual differences are vast in terms of how, when, and where to write. There are no absolutes; there is no right or wrong way to write. The writer's own needs, personality, and life stage influence which particular techniques and forms of writing are most helpful and when.

You might find it useful to designate a notebook for the journal writing exercises presented in this book. Some readers may prefer to journal on the computer or may already have a journaling system in place. Journaling in a loose-leaf notebook or on the computer allows for the addition of material to particular subject areas over time as thoughts occur.

For the purposes of this book, there are only three basic rules of journal writing. First, date your journal entries to provide a temporal context for what you have written.

Second, keep whatever you write in a safe place, rather than discarding it, even if you feel exposed, confused, or pained by it. Personal journaling, whatever you might express and however you might express it, deserves to be treated respectfully and to be available for eventual rereading if so desired. Security is key in journaling; it is hard enough for most of us to be honest with our self about our primitive, conflictual, and painful feelings without having to worry about exposure to someone else's judgment. We're more likely to be able to open up and be honest if we have trust in the privacy and confidentiality of our writing.

Third, practice benign observation, rather than harsh judgment, as you write and reflect on what you have written. You will express, and learn, more that way. For those new to journal writing, it may be wise to begin simply. On this point, Greenspan (1999) noted,

> Most people I know who use writing in the service of self-care struggle with maintaining a permissive and acceptance stance towards themselves. The territory of writing is very big; any subject is valid. You don't have to write about your client or your work, although you may sometimes find that helpful. You can begin by naming what is on your mind. . . . Begin with a sentence stem, for example, "I'm aware of . . ." Try to write steadily, returning to the stem as often as necessary. Try writing continuously for ten minutes. This is a deceptively simple way to increase awareness and promote centering. It is also likely to take you to an unexpected place. A few other sentence stems to try: "I remember . . ." "I would like . . ." "If only . . ." In time you may find your own. (p. 6)

Rainer (1978) reminded the journal reader, "You need the objective and concerned spirit of a good scientist to reread and evaluate your own diary. There is no perfect self. There is no goal. There is only the continuous process of self-completion. . . . All the efforts are necessary for they lead to the fullness of awakening" (p. 283). It is a gift to our self, when rereading our journal, to read with self-empathy and self-acceptance.

Many books have been written in the past 25 years on the how-tos of journal writing. Several authors have produced "classics" on the subject, including Adams (1990, 1993, 2000), Baldwin (1977/1991), Bolton (1999), Field (1981), Hagan (1990), Progoff (1975/1992), and Rainer (1978). The Progoff Intensive Journal Method was developed by psychologist Ira Progoff and can be used either in workshop retreats guided by trained facilitators or on one's own. It involves exercises and techniques for deepening our understanding of our interior self and to facilitate a sense of movement within our life.

BENEFITS OF JOURNAL WRITING

The psychological uses and benefits of personal journal writing, for clients and therapists alike, have been recognized by a growing number of therapists and researchers (Baker, 1988, 1989, 1990; Baker & Hays, 1986; Bolton, 1999, 2001; Greenspan, 1999; Guy, 1987; Kearney-Cooke & Rabinor, 1994; Pennebaker, 1990, 1995; Saakvitne & Pearlman, 1996; Smyth, 1998). Research has demonstrated evidence of the psychological and physical benefits of written personal disclosure, including enhanced immunity and decreased pathologic symptoms (Pennebaker, 1995; Pennebaker, Kiecolt-Glaser, & Glaser, 1988; Smyth, 1998; Smyth & Greenberg,

2000; Smyth & Pennebaker, 1999; Smyth, Stone, Hurewitz, & Kaell, 1999).

Personal journal writing can also bring professional benefits. Greenspan (1999) noted,

> By the end of a day or week, I am likely to have all sorts of reactions and thoughts inside that I have not articulated. Writing is a way to make a place for them, to discover more of what has been going on within as I saw with my clients. Writing informs me; it lets me know that moment to moment there is so much more going on than I am conscious or can express. It is a way to pause and enter a stillness within, where I can reflect upon the complexity of this process known as psychotherapy. In writing, I often make connections that surprise me and enrich the work I am doing with someone. (p. 5)

In addition, the journal is an ideal place to examine sources of and possible proactive responses to professional distress. This material can then be explored further in supervision or during therapy as appropriate.

Although personal journaling can be therapeutic, it is not a replacement for psychotherapy when therapy would be helpful. Journaling in conjunction with therapy, however, can be immensely valuable. Journaling between therapy sessions can help in the deepening of self-awareness and processing of emotion. Reading selected portions from your journal within the context of therapy may also be useful; giving voice to particular journal entries in a safe setting can be an emotionally potent, and illuminating, experience in its own right.

DREAM WORK

Another use of journaling which may be helpful to therapist self-care is to record and analyze our dreams. Journaling offers "a bridge between dreams and the waking life, a space of your own creation where the subconscious and the conscious mind meet and inform each other" (Rainer, 1978, p. 169). The general guideline is to record dream material, even just in phrases, immediately on awakening, whether on a pad kept at the bedside or directly into the journal. Three kinds of information may be noted: the content of the dream, the emotions experienced in the dream, and the emotional experience of writing about the dream. With practice in observing and writing about our dreams, we can gain insights into and deeper understanding of the material and emotions experienced through dream. Baldwin (1990) offered a number of helpful guidelines in processing dreams in a journal.

The Concept and Value of Therapist Self-Care | 1

I am amazed . . . when I give a workshop on therapist self-care, that people are so appreciative that somebody's saying it . . . It just affirms . . . that . . . I'm not the only one who's been struggling with my own needs in taking care of myself. . . . Taking care of our self . . . is not only necessary for quality of services and protection and development of our professional self—which are all very important—but we have a right as human beings, just as our clients do, to as much self-awareness, self-acceptance, and self-celebration. (Mahoney, 1997)

Why is it so hard to attend to our own needs for nurturance, balance, and renewal? Do external stresses beyond our control get in the way? Are we trying to live up to some perfectionistic, narcissistically gratifying ideal? Has self-care become another "should" (Baker & Callahan, 2000)? This chapter examines the three components of therapist self-care: self-awareness, self-regulation, and balance. It describes some practical matters we should consider when making the commitment to care for our self, and it describes the stressors that make this commitment critical to our ability to care for our clients.

Components of Therapist Self-Care

This book conceptualizes and operationalizes therapist self-care as comprising the processes of self-awareness and self-regulation and

We have a
right as
human
beings, just
as our clients
do, to as
much self-
awareness,
self-
acceptance,
and self-
celebration.

the balancing of connections among self (involving the psycho-logical, physical, and spiritual, as well as the professional), others (including personal and professional relationships), and the larger community (encompassing civic and professional involvement). The principal contributors to this conceptualization have been Jaffee and Scott (1984), who spoke of balance as an essential process in caring for one's various needs over time; Coster and Schwebel (1997), who reported evidence of self-awareness and self-regulation as the key characteristic of "well-functioning" pro-fessional psychologists; and Dlugos and Friedlander (2001), whose study of "passionately committed psychotherapists" found clear patterns of balance and boundaries between personal and profes-sional life.

SELF-AWARENESS

Self-awareness is a core element in the responsible, mature man-agement and regulation of one's self as a person and as a profes-sional. Therapist self-awareness is one of the factors significantly associated with therapeutic efficacy and therapy outcome (Frank, 1977; Mahoney, 1995; Strupp, 1996). Based on their survey of well-functioning therapists, Coster and Schwebel (1997) concluded that "Awareness is a prelude to regulating our way of life, modi-fying behavior as needed" (p. 10). As O'Connor (quoted in Ra-basca, 1999) phrased it, "Individual psychologists need to stop and look at themselves and notice their behavior and what they are struggling with" (p. 23).

Self-awareness involves benign self-observation of our own physical and psychological experience to the degree possible with-out distortion or avoidance. Only if we are aware of our needs and limitations can we consciously weigh our options in tending to those concerns, whether external or internal and whether related to personality, life stage, or circumstance. We can then consider our self-observations in tandem with information we gather from external sources, such as feedback from others received directly or indirectly.

If we are not adequately self-aware, we risk acting out re-pressed—and thereby unprocessed and unmanaged—emotions and needs in ways that are indirect, irresponsible, and potentially harmful and costly to our self, personally and professionally, and to our patients, family, and others. Unless we are aware of our self needs and self dynamics, we may unconsciously and unintention-ally neglect our patients or exploit them to meet our own needs for intimacy, esteem, or dominance.

Being self-aware is not always easy or pleasant. It involves becoming conscious of our internal conflicts and the tensions that exist between our different kinds and levels of needs. Sometimes the content of our impulses and feelings may seem very raw, primitive, and threatening to our view of our self.

SELF-REGULATION

Self-regulation, a term used in both behavioral and dynamic psychology, refers to the conscious and less conscious management of our physical and emotional impulses, drives, and anxieties. Regulatory processes, such relaxation, exercise, and diversion, help us maintain and restore our physiological and psychological equilibrium. Our sense of well-being and esteem is closely related to the level of mastery of our self-regulation and impulse control skills. Difficulties in self-regulation often cause frustration or shame.

Managing our affect, stimulation, and energy as we navigate our professional and personal lives, as well as our relationships with self and others, is no easy task. To regulate mood and affect, we must learn how to both proactively, constructively manage dysphoric affect (such as anxiety and depression) and adaptively defuse or "metabolize" intense, charged emotional experience to lessen the risk of becoming emotionally flooded and overwhelmed. Adaptive modulation between different self or ego states is also important in the service of self-integration.

Managing the stimulation we receive—in terms of type, amount, timing, and frequency—is necessary both to our internal, psychological experience and in our worldly pursuits (such as food, drink, work, family, friends). A fine line may exist between stimulation that is nourishing and enriching and stimulation that is overwhelming and stultifying. The optimal level of stimulation is optimal depends on our personality, developmental stage, and circumstantial needs. Our goal is to learn what we need to do to keep our self on course—that is, to develop our own internal gyroscope. Our ability to self-regulate increases when we are self-aware of our feelings, needs, and limits and when we practice managing dysphoria and intense emotions.

BALANCE

A positive connection and relationship with our self, with others, and with the universe serve as an antidote to the anxieties of the human condition (Treadway, 1998). A mass of empirical literature is emerging that corroborates long-held folk wisdom on the benefits of relationships and spirituality. Balance is essential in enabling us to tend our core needs and concerns, including those of the body, mind and spirit; of the self in relation to others; and in our personal and professional lives. Balancing can involve many factors, such as time, energy, and money.

The philosophical perspective of dualism is especially relevant to the concept of balance. *Dualism* refers to the presence and interactive complexity of opposing forces in ongoing tension with one another. The interaction between nature and nurture, or between mind and body, are two such dualisms underlying and affecting therapist self-care. We continually balance dualisms, consciously and unconsciously, in many spheres of life: action and rest; doing and being; past and present; self-awareness (uncovering) and self-regulation (coping), routine and variety, spontaneity and structure, primal desires and civilization, work and play, form and function, and openness and protectiveness, to mention a few.

The goal of balance is commonsensical, frequently cited advice. It's an ongoing process to learn, find, practice, maintain, and regain our balance. Balance is actually a high-level function involving modulation and oscillation. The process entails searching for the center on the continuum between the extremes. It involves dealing with trade-offs, costs and benefits, pros and cons. Fortunately, the payoffs of balance and modulation are potentially high, including a sense of mastery, esteem, and self-trust in a capacity to care for one's self.

> You can't be working at the boundaries without a sense of the center. To me, that's what life is ... always in movement and often off-balance a little bit.

"Slowly, slowly over the years, I've begun to realize that you can't be working at the boundaries without a sense of the center. To me, that's what life is . . . always in movement and often off-balance a little bit. You never quite attain the static equilibrium which, of course, would be the end of life if you did . . . but learning to catch myself at earlier and earlier moments of leaving center, and coming back to that." (Mahoney, 1997)

JOURNAL ENTRY

- ✎ Record your reactions, thoughts, and feelings regarding self-care as presented in this chapter.
- ✎ What does the discussion of the processes of self-awareness and self-regulation bring to mind?
- ✎ How do you react to the call to balance your needs with respect to mind, body, and spirit? your personal and professional lives? your connections with self, others, and the universe?

✎ Record your own definition of therapist self-care, and describe the similarities and differences between your perspective and that presented in the book.

Committing to Self-Care

RESPONSIBILITY OR INDULGENCE?

As therapists, we know the need, benefits, and process of self-care. We know that self-care is a healthy, self-respecting, mature process. We work diligently to assist our clients in caring for themselves. Therapists as a group share a consensus regarding the need and value of caring for ourselves as well as our patients (Courtois, 1999; Farber, 1981; Freudenberger & Kurtz, 1990; Goldberg, 1992; Guy, 1987; Mahoney, 1997; Norcross, 2000; Sussman, 1992). As Sussman (1995) put it,

> It may appear rudimentary to state that therapists need to pay adequate attention to their personal lives. The physical inactivity, relative passivity, and emotional deprivation that characterize the work of psychotherapists must be counterbalanced in their outside activities and involvements. (p. 257)

We need to replenish if we are to share with others. We require both physical and psychological nourishment and rest to restore our well-being and to give what we want to give—to our patients, as well as to the significant others in our lives. Self-care thus is different from selfishness, self-absorption, or self-indulgence (Domar, 2000). Self-preoccupation is, in fact, more likely to occur as a result of inadequate self-care over time. Appropriate self-consideration is a manifestation of a healthy respect for one's self and one's clients. It is, in turn, in the service of a robust, autonomous self.

> "I need to feed myself and nurture myself and value and honor myself. . . . That's what self-care is . . . remembering that I have a self. . . . Then I'm alive, I'm well. . . . I can help another person, . . . listen to him or her . . . in a way that they can then . . . hear." (Hadler, 1996)

Given the fine line between the therapist's personal and professional self, self-denial or self-abnegation is neglectful not only of real self needs, but ultimately of patient care. Iatrogenic effects (that is, harm to patients caused by the therapist or therapy) are always unfortunate, particularly to the degree that they are pre-

The physical inactivity, relative passivity, and emotional deprivation that characterize the work of psychotherapists must be counterbalanced in their outside activities and involvements.

ventable (Caplan & Caplan, 2001). Appropriate therapist self-care is an important component in the prevention of such effects.

> Regarding "the confusion between selfishness, selflessness, and narcissism . . . [t]he more I take care of myself, truly do, the more I have for others, in the best sense. And my work says that. The more time I spend . . . meditating and doing yoga, and the things that really feed me, the better able I am to be with, truly be with, the people in my office. The less I do of my own self-care . . . the less I have to give them. It's a paradox in that what we do has been labeled selfish to take care of ourselves." (Hadler, 1996).

THE RIGHT TO SELF-CARE

The reality is that therapists, as professionals and as human beings, have the right, and deserve, to share with ourselves the same time, care, and tenderness we extend to clients, family, and friends. For some of us, the idea of self-care, although rationally sound, can stimulate anxieties about the work and effort involved. It might even seem threatening: "As we psychologists address our vulnerabilities and fears and learn that psychologists are people too, we can let ourselves know that we need not be ashamed. . . . We can learn to seek support when we sense vulnerability" (Orr, 1997, p. 295).

PRACTICING SELF-CARE

As is often the case, it is one thing to know that self-care is important, but it is another to implement it. Although as therapists we are well informed about the mechanics, the how-tos, of self-care, the process remains a challenge for many of us personally and professionally. In truth, like our patients, we must learn and develop our own self-care through ongoing practice, through trial and error. As with any new learning, you may find it helpful to find good examples and models. Likewise, making a conscious commitment to "exercising" self-care can also be a proactive step.

> Regarding the pursuit of "self-knowledge, self-understanding, self-care to guard the quality or improve the quality of my services . . . I really think that it's been motivated by my own felt need for peace within myself. And much to my surprise and delight, it's spilled over into my work." (Mahoney, 1997)

There are many different ways to practice self-care. No one model exists in terms of definition, meaning, significance, or application. Differences between individuals relate to personal his-

I need to feed myself and nurture myself and value and honor myself. . . . that's what self-care is.

The more time I spend . . . meditating and doing yoga, and the things that really feed me, the better able I am to be with, truly be with, the people in my office.

tory, gender, and personality, and within-individual differences relate to developmental stage or changing needs. Such differences
influence the substance and process of self-care. For one person at
a particular stage of life, self-care might involve maintaining a very
active schedule and hiring a housekeeper. For another person, or
for the same person at a different stage, self-care might entail considerable amounts of quiet, uncommitted personal time and tending one's own home.

JOURNAL ENTRY

✎ What were your reactions as you read the section on commit-
ting to practice self-care? For example, how did you react to the
notions of responsibility versus indulgence, right, value, practice
of, and individual differences in self-care?

The Value of Therapist Self-Care

There are, undeniably, many gratifications of working as a psychotherapist. Nonetheless, the rewards of the work are also entwined
with significant responsibilities, pressures, and hazards (Freudenberger & Kurtz, 1990; O'Connor, 2000). Some of these perils relate
to the profession—that is, they are inherent in the work or a result
of rapid change and contemporary pressures within the field. Other
risks relate to our own vulnerabilities and limits as human beings
and as professionals.

Many factors influence the effects of stressors on individual
therapists. Our personal history, developmental stage, and personality as well as the potency of the individual or cumulative stressors, affect our susceptibility to stress (Elliott & Guy, 1993). "An
accumulation of stressors . . . together in some critical mass" (Kottler & Hazler, 1997, p. 194) can conceivably happen to any psychotherapist in the course of a personal and professional lifetime
and can knock even the physically and mentally healthiest of therapists off balance.

COUNTERING STRESS

For therapists, as for everyone else, stress can be external or internal, acute or chronic, situational or cumulative. External sources
of stress include contextual stimuli, such as economic, social, his-

torical, or political factors, and internal or intrapsychic precipitants of stress include anxiety-provoking feelings and thoughts, both rational or irrational. Stress responses can be stimulated by change (positive or negative), threats, losses, demands, pressures, frustrations, conflicts, and challenges (Jaffee & Scott, 1984). Physiologically, stress responses involve the release of hormones that activate the nervous system to increase alertness and sharpen the senses. Heart rate increases, muscles tense, and immune functioning is reduced.

Given the interactional mind–body connection, the sources and effects of stress overlap. The experience of physical, emotional, mental, interpersonal, or professional stress contributes to the manifestation of dysfunction elsewhere in the human system. Common manifestations of chronic stress include musculature or gastrointestinal problems, disrupted sleep, over- or undereating, decreased immunity to illness, anxiety, attention deficits, relationship difficulties, and performance impairment.

Stress tolerance, like many other human dynamics, is influenced by physiological, psychological, and developmental factors. The impact of the stressors is mediated by the potency of the individual or cumulative stressors and the characterological or developmental strength or weakness of the individual therapist. Our personal history (such as gender, early life experience, and current stress levels) also influences our ability to manage stress.

The challenges of practicing psychotherapy can have a range of negative stress effects, which have been described, in increasing order of severity, as emotional depletion, distress, burnout, and impairment.

RESISTING EMOTIONAL DEPLETION

As psychotherapists, we witness and vicariously experience a cumulative barrage of raw emotion. This can potentially lead to emotional overload as well as emotional depletion. Although not disabling, symptoms of emotional depletion include disrupted sleep, depleted physical and mental energy, emotional withdrawal from family, less interest in socializing with friends, and fantasies about mental health days or paid vacation or about being taken care of.

OFFSETTING THERAPIST DISTRESS

The term *therapist distress* is used here to describe conscious discomfort of suffering in the therapist's life. Distress "per se does nor necessarily imply impairment" (O'Connor, 2001). It might be seen or used as a warning signal. Typically, it does not preclude the therapist's working but it may potentially affect the quality of patient care, particularly if the distress is ongoing (Guy, Poelstra, & Stark, 1989; Pope, Tabachnick, & Keith-Spiegel, 1987).

Therapist distress has many personal and professional sources. A national survey of therapists has found that over 60% of therapists reported having been seriously depressed at some point during their career. Forms of distress experienced by therapists include marital or relationship difficulties, inadequate self-esteem, anxiety, and career concerns (Pope & Tabachnick, 1994).

An earlier comprehensive national survey found that work-related distress affected large percentages of therapists (Pope & Tabachnick, 1993):

> We carry our experience of vicarious traumatization far beyond our therapy space. . . . it will inevitably affect all of our relationships—therapeutic, collegial, and personal.

- Eighty percent of the respondents reported feelings of fear, anger, and sexual arousal at various times in their work.
- Ninety-seven percent of the participants feared that a client would commit suicide.
- Almost 90% had felt anger at a client at some point.
- Over half admitted having been so concerned about a patient that their eating, sleeping, or concentration was affected.

The authors concluded that these "findings are a reminder of the intense, exciting, complex, stressful, and sometimes dangerous work that psychologists do" (p. 151).

In recent years, the effects on therapists of working with patients who have experienced trauma have been referred to as "vicarious traumatization" (Pearlman & Saakvitne, 1995) "secondary traumatic stress disorder" (Figley, 1995), and "secondary traumatization" (Stamm, 1995). Like clients with corresponding diagnoses, therapists exposed to a client's trauma can develop emotional distancing or insensitivity, a loss of trust in others, increased alcohol use, or ultimately burnout. Pearlman and Saakvitne observed that vicarious trauma results in a

> transformation in the inner experience of the therapist that comes about as a result of empathic engagement with clients' trauma material. . . . We carry our experience of vicarious traumatization far beyond our therapy space. Because it changes the self of the therapist, it will inevitably affect all of our relationships—therapeutic, collegial, and personal. (p. 281)

PRESENTING BURNOUT

Burnout might be considered the "terminal" phase of therapist distress. Clinical psychologist Herbert Freudenberger (1974, 1975) is credited with first using the term *burnout* to describe therapists who were spent and no longer effectively functioning. Freudenberger (1984) defined the term as "a depletion or exhaustion of a person's mental and physical resources attributed to his or her prolonged, yet unsuccessful striving toward unrealistic expectations, internally or externally derived" (p. 223).

Associated symptoms include "fatigue, frustration, disengagement, stress, depletion, helplessness, hopelessness, emotional drain, emotional exhaustion, and cynicism" (Skovholt, 2001, p. 107). Maslach & Jackson's (1981) Burnout Inventory assesses burnout in terms of emotional depletion; detachment from other people, particularly the recipients of one's service; and a decline in feelings of personal competence and achievement in one's work.

Causes of burnout may be systemic, intrapsychic, or some interaction of the two. Systemic factors that increase therapists' risk of burnout include excessive workload, lack of control, an inadequate reward structure, interpersonal tensions, unfairness, and value conflicts (Maslach & Leiter, 1999). Personality dynamics associated with burnout include "masked narcissism" (Grosch & Olsen, 1994) and other unmet personal or conflicting needs (Freudenberger & Kurtz, 1990).

In trying to better understand the conflicts and dynamics associated with burnout, Grosch and Olsen (1994) noted that individual therapists need to become conscious of messages they took in during childhood that may be driving an overfunctioning reflex. "Only by understanding these patterns and the ways they are replicated in current work situations" can we understant and prevent burnout (p. 111).

Developmental stage is associated with burnout; younger and less experienced therapists appear to be at greater risk (Ackerley, Burnell, Holder, & Kurdek, 1988; Sherman & Thelen, 1998). Such therapists are more likely to work on the "front line" and in high-stress institutional settings and to receive inadequate supervision.

ADVERTING IMPAIRMENT

In his overview of the etiology and management of professional distress and impairment among psychologists, O'Connor (2001) defines professional impairment in terms of "impairment of ability to practice according to acceptable and prevailing standards of care." Impairment carries with it the risk of incompetent or unethical professional behavior. Risks to and protection of the public are key concerns of the profession. At the same time, O'Connor heeds "to the extent we split off our protection of the public from appropriate and effective interventions for the professional . . . . we ensure that neither population is efficiently served."

As noted earlier, therapist distress does not necessarily mean impairment per se. However, Sherman and Thelen's (1998) survey found that therapist's distress with life events or work factors correlated significantly with risk of impairment. At the same time, impairment and unethical behavior can often, but do not necessarily, co-occur (Orr, 1997).

Clearly, professional impairment is a frightening concern, for personal as well as professional reasons. Yet it occurs. In fact, Orr (1997) posited that "we are all vulnerable to some form of impairment at some time in our professional lives" (p. 294). She added that in most cases, therapists can recover from the source of their impairment.

JOURNAL ENTRY

- ✎ What were you aware of feeling as you read about the issues of therapist distress, burnout, and impairment?
- ✎ Are these matters you have thought of infrequently, or more frequently at certain times?

Therapist Self-Care Needs Across the Lifespan

2

As I have aged, I have discovered physical changes. You come to accept these things. But in the mental domain, where you don't know about what to anticipate, it can creep up on one and create a lot of stress, a lot of anxiety. . . . it would be valuable for psychologists, perhaps through continuing education, to know what those stages are and to recognize that what they may be experiencing at a particular time is a reaction to a change occurring within them, as a consequence of aging. (Schwebel, 1997)

Self-care needs change over time. As we move from youth to middle age to advanced age, our self-care must evolve to support our developmental needs. Likewise, our self-care needs when we start out in psychotherapeutic practice differ from those we need as more experienced practitioners. The process of becoming more attuned to and responsible for one's self is, in fact, developmental. It involves a gradual transition from functioning in a dependent, unconscious, childlike state to a more autonomous, conscious, adult mode. As the benefits and gratifications begin to accrue, the practice becomes more rewarding. The increase in esteem that usually accompanies self-mastery and regulation is yet a further reinforcement.

A significant body of literature on the lifespan perspective has evolved in the recognition that "the person is continually changing, evolving, growing and becoming" (Jaffe & Scott, 1984, p. 130). This perspective can help us analyze the process of becoming ourselves, personally and professionally, and can help us reflect on and anticipate challenges and difficulties over our lifetimes (Berger, 1995).

Psychotherapists share the developmental issues and concerns common to most people, but they also experience developmental challenges uniquely related to the role of being a psychotherapist and the practice of psychotherapy (Goldberg, 1991; Guy, 1987). Personal and professional stages of development may, or may not, correlate for each individual therapist. For example, therapists who enter the profession as a second career in midlife share the personal developmental needs of their age cohort but have the professional developmental needs of beginning practitioners. Each stage of development, and each combination of personal and professional stages, has its own attendant needs and challenges in terms of self-care. Coster and Schwebel (1987) described the flow of life span issues for psychologists: As persons, psychologists

> are subject to positive and negative experiences at various points in their lifespan. . . . These affect their early temperamental style and evolving mind, personality, and value system. They go through a series of potential crises in life, emanating from their own developmental changes from which they emerge either strengthened as a result of the resolution of contradictions or weakened as a result of heightened conflict. . . . The goals of any given period interact with social-historical changes. When they become psychologists, their studies and academic degrees do not shield them from the stresses of developmental changes of everyday living. They experience successes and failure, love, and rejection and they have to adapt to societal changes in family life, gender roles, marital relationships, and economic conditions. (p. 6)

The literature offers a number of psychosocial life-stage models, including Erikson's (1950) eight-stage model and Levinson's (1978) 10-stage version. The following discussion considers personal development in terms of three major adult stages: early adulthood, middle adulthood, and later adulthood.

Regarding professional development, Skovholt and Ronnestad (2001) offered a sophisticated eight-stage model drawing from Erikson's eight stages of developmental tasks across the lifespan and Kohlberg's (1967) six stages of morality development. The discussion that follows uses Goldberg's three-stage conceptualization, including the beginner, journeyman, and seasoned professional, plus an additional fourth stage, professional retirement.

Personal Development: Early Adulthood

As early adults we explore, with the vigor of youth, various sources and means of personal and professional gratification. Career development can involve an immense amount of energy and focus. Most of us are unpartnered and juggling the excitement and frustration of dating while looking for a life mate. Some of us are young parents, with young children, and some of us even live and work as single parents. For many of us, early adulthood is both stimulating and anxiety-provoking in terms of open-ended opportunity and unknowns. Looking back on that period, it may have felt easy in terms of having less responsibility, but hard in terms of a self, personally and professionally, still very much in evolution. Sheehy (1995) observed that young adulthood is a time for proving ourselves: "We survive by figuring out how best to please or perform for the powerful ones who will protect and reward us: parents, lovers, mates, bosses, mentors" (p. 142).

JOURNAL ENTRY

- If you are a young adult, how do you think about self-care in relation to the issues discussed in this section?
- How do you tend to your own self-care in the context of your other involvements?
- If you are looking back on your young adulthood from a later stage of life, did you give sufficient attention to your self-care at that stage?

Professional Development: Graduate Student, Beginning Therapist

When we are new to the field, most of us feel excited, hopeful, and probably quite scared at moments. Guy (1987) referred to the challenge of the unspecific nature of psychotherapeutic work and "the rather undefined, complex and ephemeral quality of psychotherapeutic endeavors" (p. 40). For graduate students and beginning therapists, the "elevated stressors of the novice practitioner" are part of the developmental process, with the "fragile and incomplete practitionerself" dealing with "porous emotional boundaries" and "acute performance anxiety and fear" (Skovholt, 2001, p. 55).

The stresses and strains of graduate school are multifold. Graduate psychology students experience significant performance demands in terms of course work, clinical practica, research, and dissertation. At the same time, the evaluation pressures are major; they can affect the course of our careers.

The issue of peer competition, seldom mentioned in the literature, is a major stressor in graduate training: "While academic competition is present in many advanced degree programs, it is especially keen among the talented and compulsive students, in the field of psychotherapy" (Guy, 1987, p. 44). It is stressful to be compared, usually subjectively, with one's peers in terms of the personality characteristics valued in psychotherapy, such as warmth, empathy, caring, authenticity, sensitivity, insight, and emotional maturity (Guy, 1987).

The intense atmosphere of graduate training, with its emphasis on psychological dynamics, can stimulate or exacerbate personal psychological vulnerabilities. Millon, Millon, and Antoni (1986) observed that for some graduate students, anxiety and fear can influence and "adversely affect a student's intellectual courage and innovative thinking, and . . . can foster a defensive and protective posture whereby a student may close off affect, interpersonal intimacy and therapeutic sensitivity" (p. 122).

Even under the best of circumstances, the intense and challenging experience of graduate training and beginning a psychotherapeutic practice bring about change and evolution in our perspective and values. And as we know, change, even positive change, can be hard.

JOURNAL ENTRY

- Reflecting on graduate school and the beginning of practice, what stressors come to mind first?
- What were your hopes and fears?
- Which habits developed as a student and a new professional benefited your self-care?
- Which have been problematic for your self-care?

Personal Development: Middle Adulthood

Midlife, by definition, means that we have had enough time and experience to develop skills in managing our self physically, psychologically, and socially and also that further opportunities remain to improve those skills. As put by therapist Judith Rabinor (2000), "Each year I live brings a heightened awareness of the time I have spent, the time remaining and the time left to keep on becoming" (p. 14). Hudson (1991) described the developmental potential of midlife:

> As middle-class adults move further into the adult years, they usually move from external injunctions and constraint to internal ones, from pleasing others to pleasing themselves; status comes more from internal rewards than from external recognition. Through introspection, self-evaluation, and reflection, midlife adults develop a sense of self that provides resilience and constancy. Mature adults learn how to restructure their lives, tending toward self-direction and individuation. (p. 123)

Accumulated life experience and a heightened awareness of the limits of time can also bring shifts in what we deem important and meaningful and our definition of success, love, and death (Labier, 2000). People in midlife often find greater satisfaction in the experience of "being," as well as "doing" and "achieving." Simultaneously, we may feel inner pressure to address unfinished business and unmastered personal issues. Shifts in our physical and psychological energy tend to make us choose activities more consciously. Maturing sensibilities, in combination with a broader life perspective, increase our self-acceptance of our human imperfections.

The flip side of midlife opportunities is sometimes referred to as *midlife crisis*. In Western, technological cultures, in which youth and newness are idealized, any signs of aging, as midlife signals, stir anxiety. Awareness of mortality and impending loss—of time, opportunity, health—may drive needs for fulfillment of unknown, repressed, or conflictual needs. Some "midlife crises," however, entail the breakdown of more cumbersome, early learned, eventually inefficient psychological functions or defenses, which may motivate us to explore more adaptive and mature coping mechanisms.

Midlife may also include the burden of accumulated responsibilities and commitments, personally and professionally. The "sandwich generation" must deal both with young children and with aging parents, leaving less time and energy for personal and marital relationships and needs. In middle age we typically confront the painful and significant milestone of the death of our parents. Health concerns and problems, including hormonal fluctuations, the intensifying of chronic conditions, and even terminal illness, also come to the fore.

> **Awareness of mortality can serve to motive us to live life more truly.**

In the course of midlife, the relative briefness of life becomes more conscious. We may feel more pressed to come to terms with the limited time remaining to resolve discrepancies between aspirations and actualities, for example, in wealth, status and influence, and inner and interpersonal conflicts. Yet our awareness of the limits of time can direct our choices toward maximizing life satisfaction and fulfillment. Awareness of our mortality may liberate us to live more fully and deeply, to "get real," to be more honest, to become more whole. "This awareness of mortality can serve to motive us to live life more truly" (S. Mikesell, personal communication, March, 1999).

JOURNAL ENTRY

- ✎ Has midlife often offered you opportunities to feel more clear about your self?
- ✎ What challenges to your self-care have continued or emerged during this period?
- ✎ What desires and goals are you aware of?
- ✎ If you are looking ahead to or back on midlife, what issues came to mind as you read this section?

Professional Development: Journeyman

Journeyman is the term Goldberg (1991) used to describe the therapist who "has been in the field for a while" (p. 310). The term has a long history of referring to experienced and reliable work and is useful in spite of its unfashionable reference to only one gender. According to Skovholt and Ronnestad's developmental schema (2001), the central task for the practitioner accruing professional experience beyond gradation is of integrating what was learned from others with the therapist's own personal style, of becoming more "indicated" professionally.

> Satisfaction is a common practitioner emotion at this stage. It seems to result from all the effort over the years that has now produced a practitioner who feels competent at many complex professional tasks and is paid, at a modest level or above, for the work. Those who have entered that career field to change the world either have left the work out of frustration or have modified their expectations. (p. 44)

At the same time, once reaching the journeyman stage, personal disenchantments and "cracks" or vulnerabilities may emerge.

The reality of the limits of time begin to be more apparent. Our energy may wane. Multiple role conflicts between personal and professional life may become more burdensome.

For journeymen practitioners, generativity issues may become more salient, such as a need to "give back" or leave a legacy in some way. When profession has been a primary form of generativity, we may desire to make professional changes that mirror what would have been the "empty-nest" years had there been children. There may be a desire to do other things, to nourish other needs that may have been sidelined during the career-building years. One childless therapist commented,

> Interesting—as I'm moving out of my childbearing years, I don't need my profession as much. What I would have been putting into children, and was putting into my profession, now other things feel more compelling. I'm wanting to cut back on some of the professional activity, though it's truly been very gratifying.

JOURNAL ENTRY

✎   What issues did this discussion of the journeyman professional stage raise for you in terms of self-care?

Personal Development: Later Adulthood

Recent research indicates that, although age brings physical deterioration over time, emotional well-being tends to increase with age for most people (Federal Interagency Forum on Aging-Related Statistics, 2000). As we grow older, we become more skillful at regulating our emotions and efforts, and our clarity about what is valuable and worthy in our lives increases.

Later adulthood, like any lifestage, holds opportunity and challenge. According to Erickson's (1950) lifestage model, the final stage, mature adulthood, presents the developmental tasks of negotiating the possibilities of integrity or despair upon moving into the final years of life. This process involves the challenge of refocusing and redirecting energy into adaptive new roles, acceptance of one's life, and coming to terms with mortality.

As with each lifestage, financial security and health status are critical mediating factors affecting quality of life. On the positive side, time and experience increase the likelihood of developing a

> Interesting— as I'm moving out of my childbearing years, I don't need my profession as much. What I would have been putting into children, and was putting into my profession, now other things feel more compelling.

more true and accepting relationship with one's self, which in turn often facilitates better relationships with others. Blum and Weiner (2000) concluded that successful aging is significantly affected by "how people 'make sense' of the course of their lives and maintain a coherent sense of self" (p. 25).

On her 70th birthday, A. Covatta (personal communication, January 1998) referred to "winnowing down to what really matters and setting aside nonessentials." Poet-journal writer May Sarton (1984) reflected,

> I am far better able to cope at 70 than I was at 50. I think that is partly because I have learned to glide instead of to force myself at moments of tension. . . . I am more myself than I have ever been. There is less conflict. I am happier, more balanced. . . . I am better able to use my power. (pp. 7, 10)

Nonetheless, the reality is that losses of all sorts—gradual and sudden, physical and emotional, personal and social—continue to mount and accumulate over time. Adequate functional, social, and medical support become increasingly important, and are hopefully available. Planning ahead as best as is possible is, of course, advised. Most of us are probably grappling with our ambivalence regarding this process. It deserves our consideration and it is very much a part of self care.

JOURNAL ENTRY

- What are your hopes, as well as your concerns or fears about later adulthood?
- How might they affect self-care?
- What is gratifying about later adulthood, and what remains challenging, especially in terms of personal and professional self-care?

Professional Development: Seasoned Therapist

Seasoned, another term supplied by Goldberg (1991), describes the more experienced, mature, senior therapist. Psychotherapy is a field in which time, age, and life experience are adaptive assets to the work. Seasoned therapists have consolidated a style of their own based on their own integration of theory; in addition, they are conscious of the limits of their abilities and of psychotherapy (Berger, 1995). Mahoney (1997) acknowledged how

> I am far better able to cope at 70 than I was at 50. I think that is partly because I have learned to glide instead of to force myself at moments of tension.

early in my career, I believed that there were simple and easy cures, and 12 session turnarounds. . . . Now that I'm in my 50s, I have a very different appreciation for life stages. I try to meet the client where they are rather than bring them to where I am. That feels much more comfortable and much more respectful.

In a survey of risks, rewards, and coping strategies of therapists, older and more experienced clinicians reported fewer perceived hazards (Kramen-Kahn & Hansen, 1998). A review of the literature found that

more experienced clinicians have a greater degree of comfort, flexibility, and confidence in stressful situations. . . . Experienced therapists have a more flexible, idiosyncratic, and differentiated style, and appear to be more sensitive to their own negative countertransference feelings, and thereby tend to reduce anxiety and discomfort as well as risks to themselves. (Freudenberger & Kurtz, 1990, p. 465)

More mature therapists generally become more efficient with their time, which is fortunate because other life involvements often increase and energy gradually decreases. We are less likely to choose or to feel able to work long hours on a regular basis; partly for that reason, the risk of burnout seems to lower with age (Berkowitz, 1987).

Certainly there are major issues for the aging therapist in terms of self-perceptions and other-perceptions, including concerns about competency, dependency, and loss (Blum & Weiner, 2000). Strauss (1996) acknowledged the struggle of dealing with "anxieties about the inevitable diminishing of my abilities of sensitively attending and of cognitive functioning." At the same time, she spoke of the deep satisfaction she reaps from seeing herself continue to grow, "happily anticipating the improvements in my work to come" (p. 294).

JOURNAL ENTRY

✎ How has your own growth influenced and been influenced by your professional self-care over time?

✎ What self-care struggles are you experiencing or anticipating as an older therapist?

Retirement

Eventually, all therapists terminate their practices one way or another. For some of us, retirement may be an official occurrence,

> Early in my career, I believed that there were simple and easy cures, and 12 session turnarounds. . . . now that I'm in my 50s, I have a very different appreciation for life stages.

marked by a major change from working to retired status. For others, the change may be gradual. Whether we retire early or late, to take up another career or to rest, anticipation and planning are the keys to a successful transition for ourselves and for our patients. Ideally, financial planning has occurred over time. A robust sense of self, personally and socially, above and beyond work, obviously makes a difference as well. Hopefully, we have cared for our health as best as possible over time.

Drawing from his own retirement experience, Parloff (1999) acknowledged how the therapist is often "initially reflexively concerned that the loss of her/his patients would mean giving up an important source of gratification" (p. 3). At the same time, retirement offers both challenge and opportunity in terms of meeting personal and interpersonal needs.

Lindner (1990) concluded, from observation and experience, that

> those [therapists] whose individuation is complete; who are not limited by unresolved needs to control their environment and environmental figures; and who can introspectively and honestly analyze their fantasies, dreams, desires, and emotional needs are of course in the best position to successfully handle new demands of a newly structured life. (p. 566)

JOURNAL ENTRY

✎ What thoughts and feelings, however crude or unformed, come to mind when you contemplate the issue of your own retirement as a therapist?

Growing Across the Lifespan

A broad range of options for professional and personal stimulation are available (Dlugos & Friedlander, 2001; Goldberg, 1991; Kramen-Kahn & Hansen, 1998; Norcross, 2000). Depending on personality and life stage, therapists can benefit significantly from taking advantage of these opportunities throughout their lives. The following are a few of the many possibilities:

- continuing education—formal and informal training;
- professional collaboration, such as cotherapy or writing projects;
- mentoring of new professionals;

- practice expansion (see American Psychological Association, 2001);
- development of new or untapped markets (Ackley, 1997);
- role redefinition, such as becoming a coach or an "applied life span developmental consultant" (Kovacs, 1997, p. 4);
- writing for publication or journal editing (Cantor, 2001);
- conference development (for example, Brenner, Donovan, Dubner, & Lovett, 1999, organized a conference titled First Annual Conversation Between the Arts and Psychotherapy); and
- role expansion (for example, Riskin [& Rintels, 1990] drew on her experience as a therapist to produce the award-winning television film *The Last Best Year*).

Professional and personal growth workshops are another form of stimulation and renewal. In recent years, a number of workshops focusing specifically on therapist self-care have been offered locally and nationally, sometimes as part of larger conventions, sometimes as single workshops (see, for example, Kearney-Cooke & Hill, 1994; Moore, 2001; O'Hanlon, 1999).

JOURNAL ENTRY

- What forms of stimulation have served you well to date? What have you learned about your needs for professional stimulation?
- What other forms of stimulation might you wish to try?

Tending to Our Self | 3

The life of the psychotherapist expresses a unique interplay between "becoming" and "being," as the practitioner commits himself or herself to the lifelong task of personal growth and the ongoing development of self and others. This striving for actualization reflects both a sense of duty and an inner passion, a calling and destiny. (Guy, 1987, p. 293)

A fine, but critical, line exists between our personal and professional selves. That our personal life serves as the undergirding and infrastructure of our professional self is a fundamental assumption in advocating therapist self-care. Therefore, we must strive to understand the different aspects of and influences on our self as well as to continue developing self-awareness.

Striving for actualization reflects both a sense of duty and an inner passion, a calling, and destiny.

Consciously becoming self-aware enables us to evolve from an unconscious, externally dependent, reactive mode to a more "mindful" means of caring for our physical, psychological, and spiritual being. By nurturing our self, we can then genuinely care about, and share with, others. This chapter guides therapists in examining aspects of our self, the influences of our formative and ongoing life experiences, and our motivations to become a therapist. A therapist self-care questionnaire is found in the appendix at the end of this chapter. Responding to this questionnaire and completing the journaling exercises in this chapter will offer you an opportunity to reflect on your own thoughts, feelings, and behaviors related to therapist self-care.

JOURNAL ENTRY

✎ Is the notion of further developing your self-awareness appealing?

37

✎ Are you already involved in that process?
✎ Is it uncomfortable in any way?
✎ Have you ever gotten stuck in the process?

Early and Ongoing Influences

FAMILY OF ORIGIN

The family of origin is the first and among the most formative of influences on our self. Our family history reflects a unique interaction of nature and nurture, genes and family dynamics (Titelman, 1987). Many of us have intense feelings about growing up in our family of origin, and our understanding of that experience evolves over time.

Family dynamics are often transmitted across generations, consciously or unconsciously (Titelman, 1987). Therapists are raised by parents who, despite good intentions, have their own psychological and physical limitations, including personal wounds, less-than-mature defenses, and restricted opportunities for personal and professional development. Birth order is another family-of-origin factor. Guy, Poelstra, and Stark (1989) conducted a national study of psychotherapists and found that one half of psychotherapists surveyed were either an only child or were a first born child.

JOURNAL ENTRY

✎ Make note of your feelings and thoughts about your early and ongoing family-of-origin experiences.
✎ How has birth order affected that experience?
✎ Describe how your feelings and thoughts about your family of origin have evolved over time.

HISTORICAL COHORT

Therapists, like others, are influenced by the historical forces of their generation. Wars, economic extremes, birthrate fluctuations, and new technologies all mark the formation of each successive generation. Times change quickly, creating the potential for tension and misunderstanding between members of different generations. In a relatively few number of years, the United States have witnessed transformation from a predominantly rural and small-town orientation to a relatively affluent media-connected mass society.

SOCIOLOGICAL FORCES

Sociocultural and socioeconomic differences are being recognized and appreciated as never before (Comas-Diaz & Griffith, 1988; Helms & Cook, 1999; Nagayama-Hall & Maramba, 2001; Yutrzenka, 1995). U.S. culture, with its emphasis on equality, tends to avoid focusing on socioeconomic status as a factor in personal and professional development. It might be said that our mainstream U.S. culture, with its overt emphasis on equality, struggles with the influence of class, i.e., socioeconomic status as a significant factor of personal and professional development. Nonetheless, there is accumulating empirical data that "educational background, income level, occupation, status recognition, organizational memberships, cultural orientation, religious participation, geographical location, sport affiliations, and other social factors have a heavy hand in shaping adult values, commitments, expectations, reflective capacities, and aging patterns" (Hudson, 1991, p. 122).

Sociocultural factors relate to the shared knowledge, beliefs, and behaviors of any ethnic, religious, or other social group. Social and cultural background and identification with a particular group potentially influences our orientation to self-care in myriad ways. One cultural value that influences self-care is selflessness versus self-consideration. People who value the former may place the needs of the group over their own needs. As Sapienza acknowledged (1997), "I have never learned how to care and how to nourish myself, for I had been trained to believe that this would be selfish or that there is no time for this when there is so much else to handle" (p. 5).

Other sociocultural factors that can affect therapist self-care involve the significance and involvement of the nuclear and extended family, as well as the meaning of work. Cultural attitudes differ about work as a source of sustenance or a measure self-worth, such as the use and value of time spent not working and tolerance of workaholism (S. Nieves-Grafals, personal communication, March 26, 2002).

JOURNAL ENTRY

- ✎ Reflect on the influence of societal forces on your formation. What historical influences, both personal and parental, are you aware of in your own development?
- ✎ What sociocultural influences have affected your attitudes toward work and your personal and professional self-care?
- ✎ How has your socioeconomic status influenced your attitudes and behaviors related to self-care personally and professionally?

Just as our patients are affected by their ongoing life context, so are we as therapists. Most of us vacillate between being more or less conscious of the major, and at times variable, influence of gender, personality, contemporary life, and significant life events upon our lives. Yet, indisputably, these experiences have an impact on our identity, perspective, and functioning as both people and professionals.

Ongoing Life Context

GENDER

Gender dynamics are indisputably complex. Biology and acculturation are interactive and confounded. In recent years, differences in female development (Surrey, 1985) and male development (Levant & Pollock, 1995) have each become individually recognized fields of study.

The growing influence of women in the profession of psychology has been noteworthy. Within 20 years, psychology in general has seen a significant increase in the number of female students and graduates (Pion et al., 1996). A 1999 survey showed that women accounted for 48% of clinically trained psychologists, a 10% increase compared to 10 years ago (US-HHS, 2000). The "female value" of relatedness, as considered in relational theory and research (Jordan, Kaplan, & Surrey, 1990; Surrey, 1985), validates conventional wisdom regarding the capacity of women to be empathically attuned to others and to experience self-in-relationship with others.

MALE THERAPISTS

In recent years, literature has been accumulating on the subject of men's development and psychology (Bergman, 1995; Levant & Pollock, 1995). This discussion includes consideration of what is positive and valuable in men's traditional acculturation, for both men and women, and what is dysfunctional and costly. Bergman (1995) reviewed the traditional theories of male development that focus on separation of self from other, beginning with what can be an abrupt or even traumatic disconnection from the mother, or from a relationship in general, all "in the name of becoming a man" (p. 71). However, "as with women, the sources of men's misery are in disconnections, violations, and dominances and in participation in relationships that are not mutually empowering" (p. 68).

Central to the changes that a new psychology of men should generate are a new set of relations between men and women. There is a great need to resolve the crisis of connection (Levant, 1994) between the genders and to promote empathic intergender dialogue. Men and women must move toward a more empathic understanding of the other's experience rather than assuming that the other gender can or should be measured by the yardstick of their own personal frame of reference. (Levant & Pollock, 1995, p. 386)

Although both female and male psychotherapists likely arrive home tired and depleted, multiple role strain, role overload, and role conflict seem particularly prevalent for women (Zager, 1988). If the woman therapist is a single parent or the primary wage earner in her family, the balancing act may be even more stressful. Women with children at home

perform a balancing act that taxes the most capable. Married women therapists in particular are pulled in many directions. Hearing, feeling, and relating the needs of her family, and at the same time responding to her patients' needs, as well as to her own needs, she often feels that she is living in the middle of a whirlpool (Dennis, quoted in Freudenberger & Robbins, 1979, p. 282).

Be it a function of nature or nurture or an interaction thereof, women seem at risk of slighting or forfeiting their own needs in the service of others. For many women, it is extremely difficult to tend to self first when others needs are pressing. Many women acquire "learned helplessness" or forfeit control to perceived powerful others—the "women's movement" aside—out of a fear of being perceived as being too strong or controlling.

Many women have grown up with mothers who organized their lives around taking care of others, modeling a form of selflessness. Some women, including some women therapists, may continue to struggle, more or less consciously, with a conflict about the right to have a separate self or the right to take care of that self.

> If you had one of those mothers who was ironing the clothes or in the kitchen late at night—and everybody else was sitting around watching TV, and the mother was up folding towels—then you got the message that women work unceasingly! (Layden, 1997)

Like all women, female therapists have likely grappled earlier with a range of developmental risks and vulnerabilities, including loss of ease with self and extreme self-consciousness (Pipher,

> If you had one of those mothers who was ironing the clothes or in the kitchen late at night —and everybody else was sitting around watching TV . . . you got the message that women work unceasingly!

1994), loss of self-trust, and pressure to be "nice" and to please. Some have had difficulty emotionally separating from their mothers; they may have been hyperattuned to their mothers' needs in an unconscious effort to please them and make them happier (Chernin, 1994; Donovan, 1996), or they may seek to live the life they feel their mothers would have liked for themselves.

In addition, from adolescence through later middle adulthood, women deal with cyclic hormonal fluctuations and the attendant effects on mood and self experience. This challenge is heightened in the mid-40s with the advent of perimenopause.

In her book on women and self-nurturance, Domar (2000) addressed women's need to learn how to nurture themselves: "We need to shower as much loving kindness on ourselves as we habitually shower on loved ones, and even not-so-loved ones" (p. 3).

JOURNAL ENTRY

✎ As a woman, or as a man, what has your experience been in terms of tending to your self as you are in relation with others?
✎ How much conflict has this process held for you?
✎ Has age or life stage made a difference in that process?

PERSONALITY

Although life stage affects our needs in different ways, most of us experience our own personality as essentially core and enduring across time. As a group, therapists tend to be compassionate, caring, attentive, interested, empathic, understanding, reflective, introspective, insightful, curious, optimistic, proactive, respectful, able to see humor in life, tolerant of ambiguity, tolerant of intimacy, able to be emotionally and intellectually self-contained, intelligent, highly motivated to achieve, and gratified in making sense out of the abstractness and complexity of human dynamics (Freudenberger & Runtz, 1990; Guy, 1987; Strupp, 1996).

Psychologists are also often described as having "tendencies towards perfectionism." Grosch and Olsen (1995) identified a "perfectionism and the need to be compulsive about doing things right" (p. 279). Driven by either grandiosity or low esteem, many of us

> We unrealistically expect ourselves always to be at the peak of technical proficiency; to be infallible; to be emotionally available.

expect of ourselves perfection and a continued sense of achieving. These are demands that we feel as both psychotherapists and individuals in our society. . . . We unrealistically expect ourselves always to be at the peak of technical proficiency; to be infallible; to be emotionally available to our patients; to be clear, concise, and compassionate; and to present most of our interpretations in a meaningful fashion. (Freudenberger & Kurtz, 1990, pp. 466–467)

JOURNAL ENTRY

✎ Considering your own personality, what are your self-care needs personally? professionally?

SIGNIFICANT LIFE EXPERIENCES

By virtue of being human, we all, repeatedly throughout our life-span, are affected directly and personally by stress, acute or chronic, through personal or proximate experience (Slakter, 1987). Guy (1987) reported that "75% of the psychotherapists surveyed nationwide reported that they had experienced one or more potential distressing episodes during the past three years" (p. 147). Stressful events may include physical or emotional illness (Sussman, 1995); depression (Heath, 1991; Jamison, 1996; Manning, 1994); an accident or disability (Shellenberger & Phelps, 1997); aging (Strauss, 1996); the loss of a parent, of a pregnancy (Gerson, 1996), of a child (Chasin, 1996), or of a spouse (Shellenberger, 1997); other losses, including "disenchantments" with self or within the family (Freudenberger & Kurtz, 1990); person or financial reversals; a failed intimate relationship or divorce; the challenge of dating as an adult; being single if partnership is desired; coming out as a gay man or lesbian (Blechner, 1996); working as a gay therapist with AIDS (Shernoff, 1995); multiple roles; and working as a ethnic minority therapist (Lassiter, 1990).

Stress also is experienced in response to positive events (Holmes & Rahe, 1967). A healthy pregnancy, a child's birth, and being a parent have been identified as a "mostly happy crisis of parenthood" (Basecu, 1996). Too many activities or work, even when nourishing and gratifying, can be stressful.

At the same time, some negative events, while stressful, can also be reparative. In a survey of mental health workers' experience of depression, Rippere and Williams (1985) noted that "miserable and undesirable as an episode or episodes of depression may be for anyone to undergo, it is not necessarily an entirely negative experience" (p. 187). Gerson (1996) observed, "As therapists we often make clinical use of what we have fashioned from our life encounters. . . . Personal struggles with crises, sometimes enhance, sometimes limit, but always affect our clinical work" (p. xiii).

Dr. Stanley E. Jones (1992), then director of the American Psychological Association's Office of Ethics, wrote a self-disclosing journal article about a personal life crisis of his own some years back and offered recommendations on coping in such circumstances. Jones reminded psychologists to avoid the

> autopilot response during crisis . . . get consultation for your clinical work and therapy for yourself. Accept that you are human and can benefit from help. Take a critical look at your life and goals and explore the balance of work and play. (p. 34)

Whatever the source, life events and stresses influence our energy and professional focus. The type, degree, and timing of the stress, in terms of the therapist's developmental stage and psychological and physical well-being or vulnerability have a critical impact on our ability to cope. Yet, many of us know from personal experience, our empathy and ability to thrive despite major challenges are often deepened as we work through our own life challenges.

> Accept that you are human and can benefit from help.

JOURNAL ENTRY

✎ Make a list of life challenges that you have experienced, personal or professional, past or ongoing.

✎ Go through the list, noting the first thoughts and feelings that came to mind as you remembered each challenge.

✎ Check off particular events about which you sense you still have something to say. If the time feels right for writing and reflecting, allow yourself to give language to those feelings.

✎ How do you feel about how you managed the crises you experienced?

✎ What did you learn about yourself?

MODERN LIFE

The pace of contemporary life is rushed. Many people have contact with more people in one day than people a century ago had in a lifetime (Kovacs, 1997). There are a boundless array of possibilities, options, and choices in our lives, from the most mundane to the most significant of concerns.

There are costs to this speeded-up version of life. "Our brains aren't wired to 'multi-task' the way computers are" (Rosen, quoted in Murray, 1998, p. 1; APA Monitor, 1999). Many people report symptoms of overstimulation. The fast pace and information overload may contribute to emotional irritability, concentration difficulties, sleep disorders, indigestion, cardiovascular problems, and immune dysfunction. Overload increases the risk of the psychological experience of fragmentation and the loss of a more authentic, knowable, bounded self (Gergen, 1992).

JOURNAL ENTRY

✎ How have you been affected by the times in which you live?
✎ How does the pace of life affect your self-care, personally and professionally?

Aspects of Self

SELF STRUCTURE

The capacity to psychologically function, "well enough," both within our self and with others, is, in many ways, more critical to our well-being than other assets or talents. Self psychologists use the term *self structure* to refer to functions often "ascribed to the 'ego.'" The self structure is organized and stable and comprises functions that were "performed by a parent . . . [and] taken in and established within a child, so that the child is eventually able to function for him or herself" (St. Clair, 1986, p. 9).

Self psychology theory posits that the self structure is the foundation of the psychological experience of a cohesive sense of self, or in more general terms, a sense of psychic wholeness and integratedness. Functions or by-products of self structure include self-regulation, self-management, self-soothing, and self-organization. Self-regulatory abilities are critical in the service of impulse control which, in turn, is essential in the development and maintenance of healthy self-esteem.

JOURNAL ENTRY

✎ How would you assess your own self structure? Does it affect your personal and professional self-care?
✎ In what ways would you like to grow in terms of self structure?

SELF–OTHER DIFFERENTIATION

Therapist self-care, by definition, necessitates differentiation, or "the ability to be in emotional contact with others, yet still autonomous in one's emotional functioning" (Kerr & Bowen, 1988, p. 145). Differentiation is an ongoing, incomplete, imperfect process for us all, "a theoretical ideal which is never achieved" (Grosch & Olsen, 1994, p. 112). We struggle between the extremes of emotionally cutting off others who trouble us and emotionally "fusing," or taking on others' issues or projecting our own issues onto others (Kerr & Bowen, 1988).

Psychodynamic theory attributes differentiation deficits to the early parent–child relationship. As explained by A. Miller (1981), if the infant or child senses that his or her self needs would threaten or jeopardize the relationship with the parent, adequate separation is impeded. The child

> cannot separate from his parents, and even as an adult he is still dependent on affirmation from his partner, from groups, or especially from his own children. . . . He cannot rely on his own emotions, has not come to experience them through trial and error, has no sense of his own real needs, and is alienated from himself to the highest degree. (p. 14)

According to Sussman (1992), therapists as a group tend to struggle with vulnerabilities in terms of appropriate self–other differentiation. Our level of self–other differentiation has major implications for our work as therapists, of course. Ablow's (1992) view is that "It is an essential part of my job to be aware of how my personal history might affect my response to hearing a patient's story. . . . Recognizing these transplanted emotions and their roots helps to prevent them from silently directing therapy" (p. 50). In addition, if we fail to maintain appropriate differentiation from our clients, we run the risk of countertransference, or projective identification onto the patient. That is, we may project our needs onto a patient and then, in turn, base treatment on our own covert needs rather than the patient's actual needs.

Many of us have conscientiously worked at self–other differentiation. Yet under stress, we are likely to reflexively return to earlier ways of being, which may well include some degree of self–other fusion. Some of us may still grapple, more or less consciously, with whether it is actually alright to have a separate self instead of a merged or enmeshed self, particularly if differentiation has been discouraged within our family of origin or cultural group.

If we fear losing social approval or being judged negatively for being self-serving or self-indulgent, we will be reluctant to practice self-care. If achievement and performance are valued at all costs, self-care will likely be neglected.

JOURNAL ENTRY

   ✎ What is your self-assessment in terms of self–other differentiation?

   ✎ What factors and situations support your being more able to differentiate your self from others?

   ✎ Under what circumstances might you be more likely to revert to a more merged, more confused experience?

DIFFERENT LEVELS OF THE SELF

Winnicott (1965) distinguished between the "true" and the "false" self. *True self* refers to the whole and spontaneous self, including each individual's unique constellation of feelings and abilities, preferences, affinities, and tastes. *False self* describes a compliant self that forgoes true self needs as a defensive reaction to psychic threats or wounds.

Public self is sometimes used to describe the parts of self we present to outsiders. Most of us present a version of our self to others that is a limited, more acceptable, version of our true self. This variation in how we present our public and private selves may reflect an appropriate consideration of others' feelings, but also likely favors the parts of our self of which we are more, versus less, accepting. If the difference is too great between our public and private self, it is only a matter of time before the public facade slips or falls, stirring anxieties of exposure. Freudenberger (1984) described the stress, and costs, when therapists feel caught in

> Perfection disallows vulnerabilities, weaknesses, and needs for affection and understanding. Therapists often become trapped, unable to recognize and attend to feelings of loneliness and isolation.

the role conflict between maintaining absolute professional competence on the one hand and acknowledging personal fallibility on the other. Perfection disallows vulnerabilities, weaknesses, and needs for affection and understanding. Therapists often become trapped, unable to recognize and attend to feelings of loneliness and isolation. Instead, they attempt to demonstrate maximal competence at all times and find it increasingly difficult to maintain the facade of being in charge. (p. 226)

Coming to know our true self involves being honest with our self, about our self. When we honestly consider our own needs, affinities, preferences—and limits—we feel more whole, integrated, and efficacious, as opposed to split, fragmented, and impotent. Being more conscious of our true self allows us a fuller, deeper experience of life—whatever that might mean for each of us. Although living life according to our true self may not be easy, with practice, we usually can manage well enough in the world. At the same time, we do ourselves a favor when we find settings —in both our personal and professional lives—where our true self is accepted and valued, where we can feel loved for our true self, and where we can practice being with and sharing our true self feelings.

Becoming more true and solid within our self enables us to be less dependent on others' approval or validation. Paradoxically, as we are more true with our self and others, we often become more attractive to others.

JOURNAL ENTRY

✎ What are your responses to the notion of "true self" and "false self"?

✎ How well do you feel you know and live your true self?

✎ What stimulates the emergence of your false self?

✎ What helps you reconnect with your true self?

✎ How would you describe the degree of difference between what you share openly and what you do not?

✎ Does this difference feel appropriate or problematic?

✎ Has it been your experience, or not, that your true self is appealing to and appreciated by others?

PRESENCE WITH SELF

Therapist Presence

Therapist presence is sometimes described in terms of the therapist's capacity to "listen deeply" that is, to "listen empathically, a caring attitude, warmth, compassion, and commitment to patient's welfare" (Strupp, 1996, p. 1017). Therapist presence has been identified as one of the key factors associated with therapeutic efficacy and therapy outcome (Frank, 1977; Mahoney, 1995; Strupp, 1996; Welt & Herron, 1990). It has been said that the capacity to be emotionally present, when combined with sound professional training, makes for the best of therapists.

> What I like most . . . I love when I can be quiet enough and contain my own fears and anxieties when I have something on my mind. . . . If I can just be quiet and stay tuned in . . . somehow at those times, something surprising happens. . . . They [the clients] say something I could never have thought of, but so particular to them. It's just the most wonderful thing! (Hadler, 1997).

The capacity to be truly present with others, to genuinely relate with others, including our family, friends, and clients, is based in our capacity to be in the "here and now" with ourselves. "Being present" is often described in terms of feeling more "grounded" within our self, of experiencing life "in the moment." We feel unable to "be present" when we feel dissociated from the moment; split and fragmented by inner conflict; or harassed by a harsh, judgmental inner voice or when we act out tensions through some form or degree of self-destructive behavior.

Staying present with our self is an important aspect of the self-care process. Being present with our self affords us the opportunity to observe our own feelings. Feelings and impulses are not bad or good per se; it's what we do with them, how we manage them, and how we act on them that are open to judgment by ourselves and others. Staying conscious of our feelings is not always pleasant or easy, but the benefits of giving due respect to one's self-experience are multifold. Being present contributes to a greater sense of integration and wholeness, to an increased ability to focus and concentrate, and to a sense of "brightness" (alertness, awareness) in intellectual functioning. Often we encounter a fuller, deeper experience of life, sometimes referred to as an "awakening" (Brehony, 1997).

There is value in giving ourselves time to just be, as well as to do. Most of us are more familiar with the drive to do. Treadway (1998) observed,

> Most of us lead lives that are increasingly busy. But can we say that they are truly full? How often do we feel guilty if we're not doing something with our time? And that is just the point. We have forgotten how to simply be. . . . We ensure life as human beings, not human doings. (p. 61)

> I think that many people, in their self-care practices, including myself, are drawn toward doing something that is 'good for me,' as if I can do that all in one sitting, or one massage session, or one hour of listening to music. As if I can cross that off, rather than it's being a way of being. . . . I have music playing constantly. I have a little fountain, the sound of the water reminds me of the flow, and flowing with it. (Mahoney, 1997)

> Many people, in their self-care practices, are drawn toward doing something that is "good for me," as if I can do that all in one sitting.

JOURNAL ENTRY

✎ How important has your own emotional presence been in your work as a therapist?
✎ How present do you feel you usually are?
✎ What facilitates your being able to be more present in your work?
✎ What gets in the way?

INNER WISDOM

Learning how to access and listen to our own "inner wisdom" is a wonderful gift to our self. This process doesn't preclude soliciting input and counsel from others; it involves listening to others, and then ultimately to our self, particularly the part of our self that is "impersonal, yet is not harsh" (Wittine, 1995).

> Mahoney (1997) shared his personal experience with his own inner wisdom: "I often have dialogues with 'the old man' . . . a construction of several people . . . who has unlimited time to see me . . . who does not hesitate to comfort me . . . and who at the same time has a very

realistic contact with what needs to be done . . . capable of confronting me in a constructive way, and challenging me to grow . . . [but] also attuned to my need for pacing, and to the cycles of my development. . . . I'll express whatever's going on in me. . . . I'm often quite surprised at his reactions. They're not what I would have expected. It's almost like in writing, when a character takes on a life of its own.

JOURNAL ENTRY

- Have you experienced your own inner wisdom?
- How well are you able to access and listen to this part of your self?
- What supports you in being able to do so?
- What is your understanding of the formative influences on your inner wisdom? What nourishes this part of yourself?

Motivations to Become a Therapist

Our choice of psychotherapy as a profession typically derives from a complex interaction of many factors, including innate personality and early life experience. Some motivations may be functional and adaptive; others may be less so (Goldberg, 1991). Most of us are driven by some combination of altruism (including a desire to help people in some way, to contribute to the larger society, to "give back") and more self-driven needs, some conscious, others perhaps less so (Sussman, 1992).

REWARDS OF WORKING AS A THERAPIST

The field offers many rewards, intrinsic and extrinsic, including the following:

- *Self-understanding and personal growth:* Doing therapy provides rich opportunities for ongoing intellectual growth and emotional development (Freudenberger & Kurtz, 1990; Guy, 1987).
- *Self-nurturing and healing:* In our desire to help others who hurt, we may also desire, consciously or not, to help ourselves (Barron, 1993; Guy, 1987). Perlman (1999) speculated that a "common dynamic for therapists involves a search to repair the deprivations and traumas of their own lives by

curing patients, who are seen as representing the therapists' needy child parts" (p. 60).

A recovering alcoholic therapist disclosed that

> getting into the field of psychology helped me get into recovery quicker because I had to curtail my drinking to study in graduate school. Once I got out and started working I was around people who were, by and large, a lot more health conscious . . . [which] put my own want to drink in greater contrast, so it came to my attention sooner.

- *Achievement motivation:* Psychologists put forth significant effort to earn a graduate degree, and we tend to value competency, mastery, respectability, upward mobility, and financial achievement.
- *Proving oneself:* Sometimes the drive to prove our self-worth —to our self or to others—arises out of a semiconscious or unconscious sense of vulnerability, inferiority, or inadequacy.
- *Connection with others:* Therapists may experience a form of depth and authenticity in the therapeutic process we do not necessarily experience in other familial or social relationships.
- *Reassurance and validation:* Hearing other human beings, including those who function successfully in the world, talk of their personal anxieties and their less-than-perfect lives in the privacy of the consultation office may be a source of reassurance for those of us struggling with imperfections in our own lives.
- *Organizing identity structure:* Working as a psychologist helps us establish priorities and focus our energies. It serves as a means of organizing our self and our functioning.
- *Generative gratification:* For therapists both with and without their own children, there may be genuine pleasure and satisfaction in experiencing others' growth and development.
- *Empathy or identification with vulnerability:* Our own personal life experiences may have provided us with a strong sense of empathy, or even identification, with others who feel vulnerable, hurt, wounded, pained, and undervalued.
- *Voyeurism or vicarious living:* The therapy process offers the possibility of living vicariously (Goldberg, 1991). Some therapists may be " 'voyeurs,' whose lives center on learning from and identifying with their clients in terms of excitement and fantasies about the client's life, rather than active participation in their own lives" (p. 287).
- *Rescue dynamics:* Much has been written about "rescue fantasies," particularly among helping professionals (Celenza, 1998; Sussman, 1992). Certain clients might represent (not

necessarily consciously) a parent, sibling, or part of our self
that has experienced severe pain. We may then feel a compulsion to save or rescue the other, but we risk neglecting
the patient's real experience when we react to our own dynamics (Pearlman, 1999, p. 60).

JOURNAL ENTRY

✎ What do you understand about your own motivations to be-
come a therapist?
✎ What motivations have remained consistent for you?
✎ Have any changed over time?

CARETAKING DYNAMICS

The image of therapists as "wounded healers" is widespread
(Grosch & Olsen, 1994; Guy, 1997a; Miller, 1981; Sussman, 1992).
The wounded healer archetype refers to the Greek mythological
figure Chiron, who had been incurably wounded. Through the
awareness of his own painful experience, Chiron possessed the capacity to be with others empathically in their distress and suffering.
In the process, both the wounded others and Chiron himself healed
(Nouwen, 1972). Therapists, like any other group of individuals or
professionals, vary in terms of psychological dynamics and type and
degree of vulnerability, ranging from the "human" to the more
pathological. A fine, but critical, line exists between adaptive and
maladaptive use of our vulnerabilities in psychotherapeutic work.
According to Guy (1987),

> It is the fact that such therapists have been both wounded
> and healed which enables them to offer assistance to others
> in psychic distress. . . . This wounded healer cycle is an
> ongoing process which requires that therapists possess
> several personal healing relationships in their own private
> lives. . . . These healing experiences and relationships
> provide the exceptional clinician with energy, determination,
> and perspective necessary for empowering the sincere caring
> and empathy which characterizes his or her interpersonal
> style of relating with others. (pp. 294–295)

Much research and anecdotal evidence has described one
source of therapists' "wounds": the childhood dynamics of those
who become professional caregivers. In *Drama of the Gifted Child*,
Alice Miller (1981) spoke of the relationship between early family
experience and the adaptation of characterological sensibilities useful as a therapist. She noted the correspondence between those
who choose careers as therapists and the child with a "special sen-

**Healing expe-
riences and
relationships
provide the
exceptional
clinician with
energy, deter-
mination, and
perspective.**

sitivity to unconscious signals manifesting the needs of others . . . [and] an amazing ability to perceive and respond intuitively" (p. 8).

Research corroborates that most therapists describe themselves as having responded to emotional needs in their family of origin, providing "parenting, nurturing, and caretaking for those family members who were experiencing varying degrees of physical or emotional disability, whether this involved a parent or sibling" (Guy, 1987, p. 22). One case study of 14 psychotherapist families of origin indicated the presence of at least one physically or mentally disabled family member, with the future psychotherapist being in the role of the surrogate family therapist (Racusin, Abramowitz, & Winter, 1981).

It is one matter to be considerate of and attentive to others' feelings and needs. It is quite another to feel driven and compelled to take care of others, to feel like an "involuntary therapist" who has no choice or say about how and when he or she cares for others (Jurkovic, 1997, p. 183). A dispositionally aware child in an environment of need and demand very early on learns to tend to others' feelings and needs. The risk is that this will occur before the child has had an opportunity to clarify and adequately differentiate self–other boundaries. Often, this hyper-responsiveness to others is viewed as precocious functioning and is reinforced. Praise is alluring, all the more so to a child whose own emotional needs are going neglected. Reflexive other-attuning and caretaking is a seductive, and risky, means of attempting to feel cared for and worthy.

Compulsive caretaking may appear to observers as involving a deep level of empathy or a strong commitment to being helpful and cooperative. But in actuality, compulsive caretaking is a reflexive, conditioned reaction, driven by the caregiver's own unacknowledged self needs. It manifests in an overattunedness to others' needs, feeling overly responsible for others, a compulsion to fix other's problems, and a deep hunger to be needed and appreciated. In such cases, the overt helping self covers over underlying feelings of inadequacy and dependency on external validation of one's worth. Compulsive caretaking is, in effect, "masked narcissism" (Grosch & Olsen, 1994), a reaction formation to an unrecognized wish and craving to be taken care of oneself (Hilton, 1997; Miller, 1981).

JOURNAL ENTRY

✎ The wounded healer image stirs different responses in different people. What is your own reaction to this description as it relates to you?

   ✎   What is your understanding of how your early family experiences have influenced your own caretaking impulses and behaviors?

Therapist Self-Care Questionnaire

Before proceeding further, you might set aside some time to reflect on and assess your attitudes and behaviors related to your own self-care by responding to the questionnaire in Appendix A at the end of this chapter. If you wish, note your responses in your journal. Responding to this questionnaire and doing the subsequent journaling exercise will offer you an opportunity to reflect on your own thoughts, feelings, and behaviors related to therapist self-care. There are no right or wrong responses to the questionnaire. Some parts of it might seem more intriguing or engaging than others, and you might make note of such observations in your journal. Both the content and process of this self-assessment and journaling exercise are valuable as you begin to explore ways to improve your self-care.

JOURNAL ENTRY

   ✎   What was it like filling out the therapist self-care assessment form?

   ✎   What questions stood out for you?

   ✎   Did any questions stir uncomfortable feelings?

Therapist Self-Care Questionnaire

Professional Self

Date of birth:

Work setting (for example, solo or group private practice, hospital, agency, academic):

Length of time in practice:

Theoretical or clinical orientation:

Average number of clinical hours in practice per week:

What do you like most about working as a psychotherapist?

What do you like the least?

What were your motivations to become a psychotherapist? What factors led you to choose this profession? Were family of origin dynamics involved?

What other relevant life history experiences have influenced and continue to influence your work as a psychotherapist?

Is your work as a psychotherapist different than you had anticipated? If so, how?

What real-life experiences have affected your practice?

How have developmental factors influenced your work?

What role has gender played in your work as a psychotherapist?

How would you describe the fit between your personality and your work?

How does your work as a clinician affect your emotional style and personal vulnerabilities? Likewise, how do your emotional makeup and personal limits affect your clinical work?

How do you feel your personal limits affect your work as a psychotherapist? How do you deal with these limits?

Have there been unexpected challenges in your career as a psychotherapist?

Have you experienced significant periods of professional or personal stress? If so, how did you cope? What did you learn from these experiences?

What are your current professional concerns?

How has your work situation changed in the past 5 years? If so, how?

What are your concerns about the future of psychotherapy as a profession?

Have you ever considered leaving the field? If so, why?

Therapy Self Experience: Professionals and Personals

EMOTIONAL DEMANDS AND STRESSES

What kinds of emotional demands and stresses do you experience?

How demanding for you is the emotional aspect of work as therapist?

How does your stress manifest emotionally, behaviorally, and physically?

What effect does your stress have on others?

What is the impact of your clinical work on your other relationships?

Describe your most stressful experience.

Describe your "worst fear" regarding the effects of stress regarding both yourself and others.

SELF-CARE

How do you define self-care? What meanings does the term have for you?

What are your attitudes about therapist self-care? How you think and feel about it?

Are you conscious of any conflictual feelings about therapist self-care?

Do you see therapist self-care as different from the self-care of any other professional?

What have you learned with respect to your own needs regarding self-care

- physically,

- intrapersonally (psychologically and emotionally),

- interpersonally,

- spiritually,

- psychotherapeutically (that is, in your personal therapy), and

- professionally, (such as in private or peer supervision)?

What do you do to take care of yourself as a therapist? Please be specific, and give examples.

What, for you, has been most helpful in terms of self-care? When and how?

Does your optimal level of self-care entail more time with others, professionally or socially, more time for yourself, or some blend of both?

How important is it to you to balance your life between home and work?

How do you feel you're doing at managing yourself?

What do you consider your greatest challenge in self-care?

How have your attitudes and behaviors regarding therapist self-care changed over time?

What factors encourage or restrict your self-care?

Related Questions

How do you view your levels of self-knowledge, self-understanding, and self-acceptance?

Is self-awareness something you value and have worked at over time?

Have there been particular motivations to improve your self-awareness?

Do you feel well suited to your work?

Do you feel competent, able, talented?

Do you feel gratified by your work?

Do you feel that you are growing in terms of self-knowledge?

If you could roll back time, given what you know now about yourself and the field, would you choose the same profession again?

Do you have any closing thoughts? feelings? suggestions?

I developed this questionnaire with input from the following sources: Cantor and Bernay (1992); Goldberg (1992); Guy (1987); Mahoney (1997); Saakvitne and Pearlman (1996); Sussman (1992).

Tending Mind, Body, and Spirit | 4

I talk with students who believe that when their dissertation is done . . . when they get their first job, or when they get tenure . . . then they can start doing things that they've wanted to do for a long time. My perspective is that it's important to make a commitment from the start about who you are and the way you think about your life, and the relationship between your professional life and your personal life, and be sure that you're getting something that will sustain you. (Toni Zeiss, 1996, Director of Training and Program Development, Palo Alto [CA] Veterans Administration)

T o take adequate care of ourselves, we must continue learning throughout life about what facilities, deepens, and strengthens our sense of personal well-being and peace of mind. Well-being has been described as "a feeling of vitality, of energy, of ability to do" (Jaffee & Scott, 1984, p. 152). Only we ourselves can decide what is essential to our own well-being. This chapter presents a range of issues and elements that may help us make decisions about caring for our psychological, physical, and spiritual self. Most of the topics are presented in brief form, given the limits of space. Readers may consult the reference materials cited for further discussion and detail. Thoughts and feelings that occur as you read are "grist for the mill" for further exploration through journal writing.

Tending Self Psychologically

We must remind ourselves, just as we do with our clients, that we need to stay attuned to our inner life. We benefit immeasurably in observing, without judging, our interior experience, our feelings, thoughts, dreams, and fantasies "Each person contains a vast inner world of thoughts, feelings, values, aspirations, potentials, and needs that he or she is capable of knowing and exploring. Distress, ill health, and burnout can result from neglecting this inner world" (Jaffee & Scott, 1984, pp. 129–130).

Some of us may need to learn how to better tolerate what we observe in our inner experience, particularly some of the "primary process" material, which may seem outrageous and threatening to our view of our self. Any and all of the material we observe offers us valuable information about our deep self needs. Better understanding these needs grants us more choice in how we respond or take action. For some of us, coming to recognize the existence of an interior self is exciting. It can also be scary, at least initially. With time and experience, however, a deeper connection with self usually comes to feel immensely enriching and gratifying. A mature therapist recalled her first experience, as an extern, being "taught about [the notion of] one's inner self . . . [to] understand who we are as people inside and to be fortunate enough to learn from someone who didn't pathologize, but who really believed that we are all human, we are all in it together" (Hadler, 1997).

JOURNAL ENTRY

✎ What is your own experience of connecting with and understanding your interior self?

✎ Do you desire more such access and insight?

HEALTHY SELF NEEDS

Learning to pay attention to and be respectful of one's needs, and to meet them responsibly, is a lifelong task for therapists as well as for our patients. Maslow's (1968) hierarchy of basic human needs applies to us all: (a) physiological (food, water), (b) safety (security), (c) belongingness and love (affiliation, acceptance), (d) esteem (achievement, prestige, status), (e) cognitive (knowledge, understanding, curiosity); (f) aesthetic (order, beauty, structure), and (g) self-actualization (self-fulfillment, realization of self potential). Some of these needs are purely concerned with self; other needs involve interaction and connection with others.

Maslow assumed that needs must be satisfied sequentially, but needs may also be tended concurrently. We also may feel conflict and tension between the needs of our true self and those of our "narcissistic" self (such as unresolved child self needs for appreciation and acceptance). Likewise, we may experience conflict between our needs in terms of relationship with our self and relationship with others.

JOURNAL ENTRY

- ✎ What of your self needs are satisfied?
- ✎ What needs and gratifications are more difficult to fulfill or maintain?
- ✎ What interferes in meeting these needs?
- ✎ What changes have occurred with time in your needs and your ability to express them?
- ✎ What kinds of tension and conflict do you experience among your needs at this stage, as well as between your own needs and those of others and your personal versus professional needs?
- ✎ How have these tensions and conflicts changed over time?
- ✎ What changes do you anticipate as you get older?

Healthy Narcissism

In popular culture, the term *narcissism* has negative connotations. In the psychological literature, *narcissistic disorders* and *healthy narcissism* are distinguished. The former is a result of unmet self needs (Kohut, 1971; A. Miller, 1981), but the latter refers to the ability, developed as a result of good-enough parental care, to appreciate one's own worth and to love one's self as well as others (Mahler, 1968). Healthy narcissism enables us to feel positive about our self, without needing to feel superior to, or validated by, others. Other people's appreciation and praise may be a "treat," but healthy narcissists do not depend on them as a primary source of nourishment. Alice Miller (1981) described a healthy narcissist as "a person who is genuinely alive, with free access to the true self and his authentic feelings" (p. xvi).

JOURNAL ENTRY

- ✎ Despite the obvious difficulty in being objective, what is your self-assessment of the healthiness of your own form and degree of narcissism?

Self–Object Needs

Virtually all of us to some degree enjoy being mirrored, validated, and admired by others (Guy, 2000). Kohut (1984) used the term *selfobject* to denote sources of mirroring, admiration, and appreciation. The risk to us as therapists is to rely on our patients to act as selfobjects. A. Miller (1981) warned, "The temptation should not be underestimated; our own mother seldom or never listened to us with such rapt attention as our patients usually do, and she never revealed her inner world to us so clearly and honestly as our patients do at times" (pp. 27–28).

Guy (2000) advised us to

> acknowledge the ongoing need for mirroring and find appropriate ways to satisfy this yearning. . . . Let us get intentional about our ongoing mirroring needs. . . . It is best to deliberately maintain healthy ways to satisfy our longing for respect and nurturance within a network of vibrant relationships with loved ones and friends. (pp. 351–352)

JOURNAL ENTRY

✎ For many of us, our incompletely met young self needs are either so charged as to still be relatively repressed, or, if conscious, to be shameful, anxiety-provoking, and hard to look at. What do you know about your own narcissistic self needs?

✎ What may be supportive for you in looking at and tending to these needs?

Self Time

As therapists, and as human beings, we need to achieve the best balance between the time we spend alone and the time we spend with others. The ideal proportion of self time versus other time differs between and within individuals. For some of us, or at different stages of life, time, which requires solitude, is beneficial and restorative; for others, it is essential to the health of our self.

Hudson (1991) referred to solitude as "positive aloneness . . . a quiet, deep, inner experience. . . . The capacity to be alone thus becomes linked with self-discovering and self-realization, with becoming aware of one's deepest needs, feelings, and impulses" (p. 108). Self time allows us to just be, rather than to do or to be in relation with others. It offers breathing time and space to feel, listen, and hear our self; time for whatever is meaningful; time to re-collect, recoup, and recenter. Quiet, uninterrupted time is necessary to "incubate," to think through matters of concern.

Learning, or relearning, how to give ourselves "pauses in life" (M. S. Bogner, personal communication, May 2, 2000), whether momentary or longer, is essential to our self-care. Enough personal time is important for almost everyone, but especially so for people who, although they may thoroughly and deeply savor social experiences, need time alone to replenish and restore themselves.

> I can get a lot of peace in about 5 or 10 minutes of thinking something through.

Consciously building in self time at various points in the day is a valuable self-care practice. Ziegler and Kanas (1986) suggested that health care professionals "set aside an hour as 'inviolate' and relax, walk, run, meditate, or otherwise get it together" (p. 180). Despite a daunting work schedule, Zeiss (1996) spoke of her goal of continuing to set aside what she refers to as "sacred time" for herself and her psychologist husband on the weekend. Another psychologist states, "I can get a lot of peace in about 5 or 10 minutes of thinking something through" (Gray, 1997).

> I came to the point in my life where I had to do a piece of work for myself. . . . That took every bit of extra energy I had, and more. I had to leave an elected office to. . . . The outcome for me is really having much stronger sense of self. I think that's part of why I need now to have more time, for myself, to know who I am and to really honor that self. I'm much less willing to engage in situations . . . that don't feed that need for inspiration, creativity, or understanding. . . . Whether it's age or experience . . . I can't right now get enough time and space for my own thoughts and feelings. . . . I guess I'm afraid to need what I give other people, in terms of staying with myself long enough, to break though what is established or dictated by other people . . . so I can know deeply what is in me and put it into some kind of form—through writing and poetry. (Hadler, 1997)

We can also borrow from religious and meditation practices. A tradition of "observing the quiet," in the service of connecting with one's self and the greater whole, is part of the Friends Quaker Society. It is also part of the meditation process associated with the Progoff Intensive Journal method.

JOURNAL ENTRY

- How do you feel about the amount of time you allot to your self?
- Does it seem adequate?
- If not, how do you feel about giving the matter some further consideration?
- What possible conflicts, psychological or external, might compromise your feeling able to find or grant yourself more self time?

FINDING MEANING AND PURPOSE IN LIFE

The quality of our life is deeply affected by the degree of purpose and engagement we feel at any given time (Cherniss, 1995). "People who cope well with stress have a sense of meaning and purpose in their lives" (Jaffee & Scott, 1984, p. 14). Some of what we experience as important and compelling may change over our life-span. Thus, there is value in conscious, periodic consideration of what we find significant, what has priority, and what most deserves care and protection in our lives, both personally and professionally.

The process of increasing our sense of meaning and purpose in life involves defining "success" and making hard choices in light of the very real limits of time and energy. When activity is meaningful and consistent with personal principles, we are more likely to experience satisfaction and pride in our accomplishments (Maslach & Leiter, 1999).

Doing what we can to gain perspective is helpful in understanding the ebb and flow of existence. A seasoned therapist, Canter (1998), shared about what is beneficial for her in that process:

> I find that one of the most helpful things I can do for myself is run away to a very special place . . . we have in the woods . . . when I need to think, to give myself time to feel and to heal. After a while there, it is easier to gain some perspective about a problem . . . [to determine whether] the problem requires acceptance [or] action. (p. 3)

Sometimes life events, even those that disrupt or ravage our sense of meaning and purpose, bring them into clearer focus. Creative literature offers examples of people who have found solace and fortitude amid traumatic disruption and devastation by consciously tending to the small tasks of daily life (Solzhenitsyn, 1968) or by finding new meaning in the process of surviving and growing beyond major trauma and loss (Frankl, 1969). A prematurely widowed psychologist spoke of the death of her husband in his middle age:

I imagine myself at 80. What might I hope to have accomplished with my life? From now, it is to keep focused on values and priorities.

> I wasn't ready for that. It was a shock. It's probably a gift, too. It enabled me to look at priorities in my life, at what is important. I imagine myself at 80. What might I hope to have accomplished with my life? From now, it is to keep focused on values and priorities, to try to learn where my greatest enjoyments come from, to get clear on where my greatest contributions can be. To balance work and my personal life." (Shellenberger, 1997)

For some, the ultimate means of maintaining perspective and assessing what is more or less important is to consider life from the perspective of its ending:

> Often I hear of people on their death bed, regretting missed opportunities to love, to savor and appreciate, to listen and give comfort, to step out . . . speak out, not holding back in

matters of truth and justice. . . . When I leave my body, I want to be able to say that I took nothing for granted and embraced the whole of my life with its contrasts of highs and lows, laughter and tears. That I shared my job and love with someone every day, making the world less dark and bleak. . . . I want to ask my questions and state my wants. What are my passions, and how can I cultivate them? How can I mesh my individual soul with the soul of the world? (Covatta, 1998, p. 1)

JOURNAL ENTRY

- What gives your own life meaning and direction at this stage?
- What supports and grounds you in maintaining a sense of meaning and purpose?
- What is threatening?
- What is helpful for you in maintaining perspective on life?
- What can get in the way?
- What helps you regain your perspective?

Getting the Most From Everyday Life

Most of life is everyday life. We offer ourselves an immense gift by appreciating the small pleasures of the quotidian. People diagnosed with terminal diseases like cancer often report significant satisfaction in consciously experiencing the sights, sounds, smells, and experiences of life, day by day.

The practice of living in the moment, in the here and now, has been said to involve the cultivating of "ordinary magic" or "the sacred in everyday life" (Moore, 1994). A related notion is that we each have the potential to become an "artist at life" (Baker & O'Neil, 1989).

Simplicity has been cited as a prerequisite for enjoying the details of life. To live a simplified life we must let go of what prevents us from applying energy, focus, and concentration to what truly matters to our self (Breathnach, 2000).

JOURNAL ENTRY

- What is important to you in terms of everyday life—what sights, sounds, and smells?
- Do you relate to the idea of "the sacred in everyday life" or becoming an "artist at life"?
- What would you need more of in your everyday life to appreciate the sacred or be such an artist?
- Note what comes to your mind on the subject of simplifying your life.

Taking Charge

In reality, each of us has minimal control over other people's lives. What we can do is to take charge and responsibility for our own lives. We can become our own authority. We can claim, or reclaim, our self.

The ability to organize and mobilize our self, physically and cognitively, can make a significant difference in our mood and functioning. A sense of personal control in one's life has been associated with more successful coping (Flannery, 1987). Studies on midlife development and the aftermath of trauma have reported a strong relationship between sense of personal control, life satisfaction, and health (Lachman & James, 1997; van der Kolk, McFarlane, & Weisaeth, 1996). Zeiss (1996) spoke of early lessons in riding the waves of life:

> You face life —and that you, in fact, not only face it, but you move towards it and dive into it.

One of the first things I can remember learning in life is my parent's teaching to never turn your back on life or you'll get knocked down. 'You can't run away from things' was basically the underlying message. You face life—and that you, in fact, not only face it, but you move towards it and dive into it. In doing that, you take control of it. You join it in a way that works. If you're afraid of getting rolled—which we all were—the advice was 'Go get rolled. Make it happen.' You know then how to make it happen. You know where the wave is going to catch you in a certain way. You learn what it feels like, learn how that works, discover that it's not fun, that you might get some water down your nose, but learn that you'll pop back up again. The wave will carry you to the beach and deposit you on the beach. There you'll [safely] be.

In our efforts to take charge of our life, the principle of gradualism is applicable. Small, steady, modulated, incremental, "no-fail," manageable steps—at a maintainable pace over time—provide both a gratifying "in the moment" experience as well as a sense of cumulative accomplishment. Writer–poet Julia Cameron (1998, p. 52) wrote of "one breath at a time, that is how life is built. One thing at a time, one thought, one word at a time. . . ."

Proceeding at a manageable pace affords many benefits over time. A modest, but steady, pace allows us to contain or reduce anxiety; it promotes focus, concentration, engagement, and consciousness so that we feel less overwhelmed and out of control; and it encourages proactive rather than reactive responses, thereby facilitating a sense of efficacy and mastery.

Sometimes "multitasking" is appropriate and doable—for a while. Yet the amount of stimuli we can effectively focus on or manage for any length of time is limited. Although it may not seem grand or exotic as a way of living life, modulated pacing helps us maintain, and regain, our sense of balance across time and situation.

Taking charge of our life also involves conscious self-organization, structuring, and planning. For many of us, "getting organized" is self-comforting and self-calming and can promote more effective rational and emotional functioning. Tending to what is controllable and manageable in life allows us more energy and time to address what is less within our control.

One of the most effective tools for self-organization is writing out plans, on a daily or weekly basis, that include the following:

- time for activities that are personally meaningful;
- organization of tasks into beginning, middle, and end stages;
- scheduling of intermediate tasks to avoid the deadline rush;
- "incubation," time for working through issues; and
- extra time to allow flexibility to deal with unpredicted problems.

A fine line exists between healthy versus excessive control. Overcontrol may be a function of lack of practice in modulation and self-regulation, or it may be a reaction formation to painful experiences with lack or loss of control. Flexible, modulated, good-enough self-organization, structuring, and planning are optimal goals. The ideal is to "plan enough to feel somewhat in control without letting the planning control you" (Sapadin, quoted in Edmonds, 1998, p. 4).

JOURNAL ENTRY

- ✎ What degree of control do you have in your life?
- ✎ Does it seem adequate? excessive?
- ✎ Does your need for control intensify with stress?
- ✎ Have you been tempted to forfeit control in a maladaptive way when you have felt overwhelmed?
- ✎ What were the consequences of that?
- ✎ What seems helpful in maintaining an optimal level of control in your life?
- ✎ What kind of pacing—personally and professionally—generally works best for you over time?
- ✎ What external and internal influences can get in the way of your optimal level of pacing?
- ✎ Are you satisfied, or not, with the quality and quantity of your organization in your personal and professional lives?
- ✎ What factors help you get and stay organized enough?

Optimizing Coping Mechanisms

Coping mechanisms are acquired, conscious means of managing impulses and anxieties. Coping skills change and vary across the lifespan, often strengthening with practice. If our coping mechanisms are maladaptive, they can interfere with and counteract our self-care efforts.

There is value in periodic assessment of coping skills in terms of maturity, reliability, and cost-effectiveness. The goal for ourselves, just as in our work with our patients, is to find the most proactive, adaptive, effective means possible of addressing the stresses in our lives. The more skillfully we can cope with our impulses and anxieties, the less likely we are to act them out.

The literature recommends the following when building coping mechanisms:

- choose "coping strategies that do not . . . carry heavy costs (e.g., addictions, numbness, isolation)" (Saakvitne & Pearlman, 1996, p. 44);
- find adaptive "prostheses" as needed, i.e., ego-syntonic means of containing immature reactions until you can develop more mature coping skills;
- develop healthy "release valves" to help minimize the buildup of disabling tension; and
- learn more about the underlying causes of "generalized anxiety" or undefined stress that you may experience.

JOURNAL ENTRY

- How adaptive would you say your coping skills are at this time?
- What form and degree of maladaptive coping can occur under stress?
- What is helpful to you in maximizing your coping?

Voice and Language

Clear communication with self and others is an essential component of self-care. Being able to put emotion and needs into words is a critical part of the self-regulation process and greatly enhances the relationship with self and with others. Being able to give language to intense emotion can help to defuse or metabolize emotion. We don't have control over what we feel, but learning to talk out—versus act out—intense, sometimes frightening, emotions can make all the difference in our lives. With others, there is a value in practicing expression of our feelings and assertion of our needs in a calm, clear manner. For example, saying "no" when necessary also helps to establish clear boundaries.

Practicing positive, constructive self-talk has value as well. We can grow, just as our clients do, in our capacity to self-soothe, self-calm, and self-contain. In effect, affirmative self-talk exercises our capacity to talk out, rather than act out, our feelings. We strengthen our ego functions and our rational, adult self in the process.

Personal journaling can be a useful part of this process. Journaling can facilitate self-management by helping to clarify goals. Journaling can also contain and diffuse tension by exercising self-modulation and self-soothing in daily life and during times of emotional upheaval or trauma.

JOURNAL ENTRY

- How do you assess your own ability to speak out for yourself?
- What can get in the way of that process?
- How might you still further develop and grow in this ability?
- Do you find positive self-talk helpful? If so, what kinds of things do you find particularly helpful to say as you talk with yourself?
- Does the way you talk with yourself make a difference as well?

Limiting Stress

Individuals differ significantly in terms of stress responses. What is stimulating to one person might be uncomfortably stressful to another. "Unhealthy stress" results when stress responses are stimulated, but effective means of dealing with the stress are precluded.

If we become overwhelmed by professional or personal stresses, we are all at risk of regressive or dysfunctional coping behaviors. Regression in response to stress may indicate inadequate or immature defenses, but it can happen even to the most emotionally developed people in response to cumulative stress and drained reserves.

If we feel stresses accumulating, we must take responsibility for getting ourselves into therapy sooner rather than later. There, ideally, we can consider the optimal management of our stresses and tend appropriately to any uncovered psychic wounds. A senior psychologist with major responsibilities in a large medical center acknowledged

> how much I count on things rolling along, having the supports underneath my work and functioning well. If that's

It's very stressful for me when I can't do everything I've committed myself to do.

happening, then I can be happy, and delighted that everything is working. But if . . . something interrupts that process, that's a big anxiety for me . . . if it feels like things are going to cave in on me, that I won't be able to keep up, that I'll start falling behind, that I might fall down. It's very stressful for me when I can't do everything I've committed myself to do.

JOURNAL ENTRY

- ✎ What is stressful to you at this stage of your life personally and professionally?
- ✎ How much is your stress coming from within yourself?
- ✎ How much comes from outside yourself, and from where?
- ✎ What is helpful and adaptive for you in coping with the stresses in your life?

Ambition—Healthy or Questionable?

Ambition can help motivate us to get the most out of life. It can also contribute to neglect of self or family. Excessive ambition, which may be driven out of a compensatory need, is often highly reinforced in the external world, but it usually depletes rather than enriches the self over time.

There is value in periodically and thoughtfully reviewing our goals and self-expectations. It can be hard to discern whether we are stretching our self in the service of growth or being driven by internal pressures that may be destructive over time. Self-awareness of that fine line is a valuable goal, particularly if we tend to push our self maladaptively.

JOURNAL ENTRY

- ✎ How well do you feel you understand and fulfill your own ambitions?
- ✎ How much conflict do you experience among your various ambitions and needs?
- ✎ How much do your own ambitions and needs and those of your family and patients conflict?

Addressing Overfunctioning and Overwork

Overextending one's self beyond one's abilities—developmentally, physically, or emotionally—is normalized within certain cultural roles but is not compatible with therapist self-care. Overfunctioning is sometimes a response in children growing up in families where the parents, for whatever reasons, are unable to function adequately enough: "Clinicians who have routinely responded to the pressing needs of significant others since childhood are at risk of unwittingly 'going beyond the call of duty' . . . of 'overfunctioning'" (Jurkovic, 1997, pp. 181–182). "Often it reappears in work settings, which all too easily become yet another family and a new arena for overfunctioning" and a setup for potential burnout (Grosch & Olsen, 1994, p. 111).

Overfunctioning may serve a number of functions. In some cases, it may be a reaction formation to a previous underfunctioning. We may overfunction to alter our mood or to divert our self from the demands of consciousness. Overfunctioning may be an effort at self-stimulation if we are feeling depressed or an attempt at self-calming in response to an ominous fear that something terrible would happen if we slowed down (Grosch & Olsen, 1994).

Whatever the origin, "This well-intended generosity is usually performed at great expense . . . the loss of freedom to be a 'real self'" (Grosch & Olsen, 1994, p. 111). Likewise, overfunctioning is likely to add to the blurring between the therapist's personal and professional life and between the therapist's and the patients' needs. "Overfunctioning is not easily overcome, not only because it's familiar, but also because it is so well rewarded" (p. 111). It is often confused with "ambitiousness" and is thereby socially sanctioned. The payoffs of overfunctioning can be quite seductive.

A variation of overfunctioning, again professionally and personally normalized, rewarded, and seductive, is what might be referred to as a "hypomanic lifestyle." It is not unusual to hear our colleagues and ourselves refer to a "packed," "crazy," or "jammed" schedule. A frenzied and frenetic life can start to feel very familiar and normal. When overfunctioning is a standard mode of operation, a dysfunctional, and eventually costly, level of stress tolerance may evolve. "A frenetic lifestyle can be both a defense against and a cause of burnout" (Grosch & Olsen, 1994, p. 131).

Overwork—work addiction or "workaholism"—is yet another form of an "altered state," a diverting from the present. In contrast to many other altered states, such as alcohol, drug, or food abuse, overwork is often culturally normalized, sanctioned, and reinforced. Yet work addiction is similar to other compulsions and addictions in that something external is being used to divert or cover over underlying anxieties and pain:

> In some families, work functions like an addiction that
> prevents underlying emptiness from manifesting itself. Like

other addictions, overwork tends to be passed on generationally. This predilection for overwork is particularly common in families who have experienced substantial loss, economic depression, or financial reversals. (Grosch & Olsen, 1995, p. 278)

Grosch and Olsen (1994) spoke of another subtle and highly normalized form of dependency: They compared "adrenaline dependency" to other chemical or drug addictions that provide an initial rush, followed by a letdown and a desire to restimulate the high:

> Adrenaline dependency . . . though technically not an addiction, a form of hurry sickness develops whenever we are caught up in a lifestyle that is pressure-filled and demanding. . . . If there is more to do than there is time to do it in, particularly if the work has some risk associated with it, adrenaline surges are inevitable. (p. 130)

> The signs include always being in a hurry with never enough time; a constant need for stimulation and excitement; feeling fidgety, restless, and impatient during times of inactivity; and generally a time of depression following a very intense and busy time. (p. 131)

> Non-work activities, including recreation, can feed the addiction. . . . If careers are busy and demanding, hobbies and activities may be chosen that follow suit. (p. 132)

The process of deconditioning this dependency involves first becoming aware of the compulsion to "keep pushing" and then practicing conscious slowing down and self-moderation. Limiting stimulation, or the amount and intensity of activity and "commotion" in our lives, may also help us stay more conscious. The process may also benefit from "scheduling periods of inactivity, and perhaps even setting aside a day to do nothing. Obviously, it also involves building adequate rest periods into our lives, and developing healthy, relaxing habits. This is easier said than done" (Grosch & Olsen, 1994, p. 132).

JOURNAL ENTRY

- ✎ Do you depend on overfunctioning, overwork, or adrenaline to get things done?
- ✎ If so, how has this dependency evolved? How costly is this dependency for you?

Managing Technology

The gains, as well as the costs, of modern technology are still becoming apparent. Many of us appreciate the convenience of voice mail, personal computers, the Internet, e-mail, electronic calendars, and cell phones. At the same time, such technologies can erode the boundaries between work time and nonwork time and create the expectation of instant responsiveness and 24-hour accessibility (Fraser, 2001).

Demands, needs and preferences regarding the use of technology may vary, "but it's important to remember that we have choice and control in what technology we use, as well as how we choose to use it" (DeNelsky, quoted in Volz, 2000). We can set aside times to use the phone machine in avoiding nonessential calls and to respond to phone messages, e-mail, and faxes. Nonemergency calls received in off-hours can be returned the following business day. Phone appointments can be arranged to interrupt phone tag. We can consciously decide whether to take our computer or e-mail on vacation or not. Scheduling time free of technology, such as during exercise, dinner with friends or family, and vacations, will ensure that important activities are uninterrupted. Television viewers can wear a headset if the noise affects others in the house. Some find it relieving to have rooms in the house that contain no electronic devices.

JOURNAL ENTRY

- ✎ What issues have you encountered in managing your use of technology, both personally and professionally?
- ✎ What kinds of changes might you make or experiment with in your technology use?
- ✎ Is there any technology that you've been intimidated by that you might want to try out?
- ✎ What would be helpful in supporting that endeavor?

Self-Care Rituals

Simple and benign rituals can be a self-calming and self-organizing antidote to the stimulating, fragmented swirl of contemporary life. Ritual can be transformative. It can offer a means of renewal for the caregiver (Kearney-Cooke & Rabinor, 1994; Rabinor & Kearney-Cooke, 1998). "Therapeutic rituals consist of prescribed symbolic acts which must be performed in a certain order using symbols. Both the symbolic behaviors and symbols themselves often have more than one meaning" (Kearney-Cooke & Rabinor, 1994, p. 4). Ritual can be used to mark transitions (i.e., a notable change from one defining life state to another) and continuity of events or times (e.g., a birthday or anniversary). Ritual can include symbolic movement and can use items representational of a significant aspect of the transition or continuity. Rhythms or sounds may also be meaningful elements: drumming or chanting can contribute to visceral–emotional experiencing of the rite.

Both repetition and variation can occur within ritual. One example of ritual for renewal might be holding a time of day, such as early morning, for personal journaling. A familiar setting, familiar paper and pen, and possibly music might be a part of the ritual. The content of journaling might well vary significantly over time.

JOURNAL ENTRY

✎ Do you have ritual in your life? in small ways? in large ways? for yourself? shared with others?

✎ Are there rituals that you practice especially to support yourself as a caregiver?

✎ Would you like more ritual in your life? If so, what form comes mind?

REPLENISHMENT

To have enough to share with others, personally and professionally, we need to nourish ourselves. The literature has repeatedly underscored the need for therapists to replenish themselves, yet we still need to remind ourselves constantly. Two decades ago Freudenberger and Robbins (1979) admonished therapists to "feed themselves in a constructive manner so that there is . . . enough coming in from outside their own professional world so that professional relatedness is not used as a substitute for adequate relatedness to the real world" (p. 290). More recently, Goldberg (1992, p. 130) spoke to the "wisdom of self-renewal," the granting to our self the opportunity to refuel emotionally and physically, to regain perspective, to regain awareness and consciousness, to allow for self-diversion and enrichment.

JOURNAL ENTRY

✎ Do you feel adequately replenished in your life personally? professionally? If not, what types of replenishment might you need?

✎ What would you need to do, and what kinds of supports might you need, to build this form of replenishment into your life?

Replenishing Activities

Pearlman and Saakvitne (1995) advocated the value of nonwork activity and hobbies as important for the "fuller expression of oneself" (p. 394). Ziegler and Kanas (1986) recommended that, as health professionals, we intentionally allot time and energy for creativity, self-expression, growth, and leisure by reading for pleasure, playing with a pet, playing sports, making music, attending concerts and museums, walking, hiking, being in nature, gardening, or simply laughing. The list of possible renewing activities is virtually limitless; one colleague found that

> Playing drums and being in a band is very renewing. . . .
> Drumming (the sound, the rhythms, the repetitive physical activity) has a physiological effect that may be related to Shamanic drumming experiences and perhaps to brainwave and brain chemistry levels. (B. C. Schlosser, personal communication, August 10, 1999)

> Art, literature, plays, movies, paintings, dance . . . where I can participate and can identify, where I'm taken beyond what I've felt or thought . . . before . . . and . . . [then reconnected] with myself. . . . I am in charge of putting myself in a situation where I can have that occur. (Hadler, 1997)

When choosing replenishing activities, the goal of recreation is to energize, rather than "numb out" (Treadway, 1998). Consider the costs of activities in time, money, or stress. Consider another activity if one becomes too costly in terms of time or emotional, physical, or financial resources. The goal is to enjoy ourselves and to let go of responsibility and burden. Some have described this as "play":

> Play . . . is a soothing balm for the soul. . . . The 'treadmillitis' of the adult work, particularly the stresses and burdens of those in the demanding mental health field, can be dramatically transcended as we let go of our grown-up persons and invite the liberating spontaneity of a playful spirit into our existence. (Treadway, 1998, p. 61)

> Part of what helps me stay balanced is playing . . . being able to be playful. . . . Maybe I'm blessed in that being playful comes so naturally to me. . . . I've allowed myself to have that part of myself. (Beer, 1997)

Our life stage and personality affect what activities and conditions we find nourishing. For example, more introverted personalities may need more alone time for replenishing compared to extroverts. Those of us who find being able to receive or to take in a challenge must consciously search out activities that fulfill these functions in a way we are comfortable with. It's a gift to allow ourselves to engage in or learn new activities where we don't have to be in charge or responsible or "to be an expert anymore. It's

Part of what helps me stay balanced is playing . . . being able to be playful. . . .

about the freedom not to know the answers and to take in rather than give out" (Treadway, 1998, p. 58).

> The way that has been the most effective way for me is to say 'yes' to things that are outside of work—like our daughter, and all that has gone with that, 'yes' to committing to camping trips, and 'yes' to planning a trip to Nepal. Just saying 'no' for the sake of 'no' doesn't work for me. (Zeiss, 1996)

JOURNAL ENTRY

- ✎ In what ways do you replenish and re-create in your personal and professional lives?
- ✎ Have your recreational needs and tastes changed over time?
- ✎ What factors conflict with your recreation needs and desires?
- ✎ What might be some proactive steps in addressing unmet recreational needs either personally or professionally?

Healthy Gratification

Adults sometimes nervously joke about whether their gratifications are healthy or legal. As humans, and as professionals, we need gratifications. The challenge is finding and nurturing positive ones.

We all start out as children being largely dependent on external sources of pleasure, comfort, assurance, stimulation, and diversion. It is easy and natural to continue to look externally. Learning how to find pleasure and gratification in healthy, proactive, cost-effective ways is one of the major tasks of adulthood. The more conscious we are of our preferences, the more we are able to shape our goals and direct our energy. Likewise, we can consciously develop "guardrails" that protect against reverting excessively to more primitive gratifications, such as food, interpersonal merger, drink, or sexual acting out. Most of us are tempted, at one time or another.

Learning how to nourish and sustain our healthy gratifications is a major gift to self, psychologically and physically, with benefits accruing over time. Fortunately, self-management is, in itself, a healthy gratification!

JOURNAL ENTRY

- ✎ Do you have enough healthy gratifications in your life?
- ✎ What risky or unhealthy gratifications are you tempted by?
- ✎ If you need more healthy gratifications, what might be some next steps toward that goal?
- ✎ If you're concerned about unhealthy gratifications, what might be helpful in addressing this matter?

Relaxation and Respites

For many therapists, "Relaxation, really, is challenging hard work. In fact, to many successful professionals, relaxation is—or would be, if they did it—the hardest job of all" (Grosch & Olsen, 1994, p. 131). Ziegler and Kanas (1986) advocated early training for health professionals to "cultivate relaxation habits with the same energy and commitment that you apply to your work" (p. 180).

The chief executive officer of the American Psychological Association (APA), Raymond Fowler, announced to the APA membership in early 2000 that for the first time in his 30+-year administrative career, he was taking a leave of absence; stress related to events had taken a toll on his health. Dr. Fowler (2000) acknowledged lessons learned: "My personal experience tells me that I have to build in more small down times to avoid a large one and that good time management doesn't mean working every possible minute" (p. 9).

A hiatus or respite from the everyday demands of clinical work is an immense gift to one's self. Holidays, vacations, and sabbaticals provide an opportunity to get a fresh perspective, and to reconsider one's needs and options. Sometimes such leaves are paid; often in private practice they are not, but the psychological and other benefits are worth the exchange in income. Obviously, short- and long-term costs and benefits need to be considered carefully. In addition, back-up coverage of one's practice by a trusted colleague, who can be contacted in case of emergency, is necessary. Typically, colleagues will develop reciprocal coverage arrangements for each other over time.

Pope (1999) shared his thoughts about the importance of time away from work for doing the quality of work he values:

> Before I'd actually begun full-time solo practice . . . I knew from my prior experience that therapy and other forms of clinical work took a lot of attention, concentration, and energy; if I were going to do solo practice for 40–45 hours each week, I'd need sufficient time off (to relax, enjoy the other, non-psychology parts of my life, and recharge) in order to look forward to this work on a daily basis over several decades. This seemed virtually essential. I decided to take 6 weeks of vacation each year. This has allowed me to work as hard as I can and be emotionally available during each session and yet not become exhausted over the years. (Div. 42 listserv, October 18, 1999)

Holidays from work may be short or extended. A minimum holiday of two consecutive weeks at least once a year is recommended and preferred by many therapists. Enough time away from the practice—from phone calls, from patient responsibility—is essential for rest and renewal.

> When I'm able to leave my responsibilities . . . in two weeks . . . I end up going into this sort of place inside of me that doesn't get explored any other time. (Munn, 1997)

Life stage, personality, and resources influence the kind of vacation chosen. Different versions of vacations offer different benefits. The continuum of options ranges from active and demanding (for example, athletically, or socially intense) to restful, simple, "organic," and quiet. Likewise, although business trips may sometimes involve travel and sightseeing, business travel is just that and is different than a holiday from work.

JOURNAL ENTRY

- ✎ Do you feel you give yourself enough time to breathe and to collect yourself during the day?
- ✎ Do you build in enough moments of appropriate relaxation in the course of your life—personally? professionally?
- ✎ How important are holidays for you in your personal life? your professional life?
- ✎ Are you satisfied, or not, by the kind or frequency of your holidays?
- ✎ What do you like to do on vacations—rest? be adventuresome? visit family or friends? travel? some combination thereof?
- ✎ What do you see desire more of with respect to your holidays?
- ✎ Have you ever taken, or considered taking, a sabbatical from your work?
- ✎ Is there something else you'd like to do, if you were to take a sabbatical from your work?
- ✎ What would it involve to further explore such a possibility?

Practicing Self-Compassion and Self-Acceptance

Therapists, like everyone else, are human beings. Each of us has our own unique constellation of vulnerabilities, imperfections, and limitations. Some of us may have difficulty appreciating our uniqueness and valuing our differences from others.

There is value, for us, as for our patients, in coming to terms with our humanness—in accepting our own unique constellation of qualities and our own personal limits. This doesn't mean we can't keep on learning and growing. It means accepting the reality that, try as we might, we will always be less than perfect, and that's all right. Learning to offer empathy, tolerance, acceptance, compassion, and realistic (not rationalizing, but rational) appreciation of our own humanness is truly a gift to our self, and indirectly to others: "It is unconditional compassion for ourselves that leads naturally to unconditional compassion for others" (Sapienza, 1997, p. 5). In some cases, learning to be self-compassionate may require us to adopt an attitude (and corresponding behaviors) that may initially seem foreign and that we may never have received or truly experienced.

Self-rejection and self-abnegation involve denial and "splitting off" of parts of the self experienced as unacceptable to significant others at vulnerable early stages of development. Later in life, such defenses drain off psychic energy and result in a fragmented, fragile sense of self. Alternatively, the benefits of genuine self-compassion and self-acceptance are significant indeed. With a greater sense of wholeness and integration, we have more energy to better meet the challenges and thereby reap the satisfactions of each stage of our life. With a stronger sense of healthy autonomy, we are less dependent on others for acceptance and approval.

> The challenge of internal acceptance, and feeling good enough, feeling at peace, feeling confident enough, comfortable enough with what I know and what I don't know, with what I can do, and don't do, and maintaining a balanced perspective of myself. That is the greatest challenge for me. (Hadler, 1997)

JOURNAL ENTRY

- ✎ How would you describe, and how do you feel about, your own unique constellation of qualities that contribute to you as an individual being?
- ✎ What are your limits, and how do you feel about them?
- ✎ How have your descriptions, and acceptance, of your individuality changed over the years?
- ✎ How do you see yourself faring in the practice of self-compassion?
- ✎ Have you observed growth in your ability to offer yourself the empathy and compassion you extend to others?
- ✎ How would you like to further grow and develop in your ability to be self-empathic and self-compassionate?

Observing Defense Mechanisms

Defense mechanisms develop beyond our awareness to protect us against psychic pain (Cramer, 2000). It is only when these mechanisms become more costly than effective that we might become motivated to look at them more consciously. Depending on the age and severity of the psychic wounds, defenses may, or may not, evolve from lesser to more mature forms.

It is not necessarily easy, or painless, to observe the ways in which we emotionally protect ourselves: "Therapists may have considerable difficulty in acknowledging doubts about their own lives and any feelings of inexpertness. . . . Denial, and its variations and derivatives, are tempting in the hopes of avoiding the anxiety of insecurity in our professional and personal lives" (Welt & Herron, 1990, p. 322). Becoming aware of less-than-mature adaptive behavior can be uncomfortable or even shameful. Displacement, self-forfeiture, repression—and other versions of immature defenses—can be hard to acknowledge. Yet with awareness, we have the possibility of undertaking needed healing and eventual growth.

JOURNAL ENTRY

- What do you know about your own defense mechanisms?
- Do their benefits to you outweigh their costs?

Discriminating Sources of Dysphoria

All human beings deal with a range of complex, multifactored stresses. It is not always easy to sort out the sources of anxious and depressed feelings. In some cases, such feelings are old, "neurotic," deep-seated conditioned responses being restimulated by something familiar in the present. In other cases, anxiety and discomfort may signal problems, potentially necessitating attention and possible intervention. When dysphoria is a result of earlier conditioning, we are left, just as our clients, with the challenge of managing and regulating our conditional reactions.

Voice and Language

Object relations theory offers another valuable insight for self-care: that we can learn to identify, contain, and confront early internalized, anti-self ("antilibidinal") messages or "introjects," which are directly or indirectly transmitted messages that we incorporated from parents or significant others. In cognitive–behavior language, we can learn to modify negative, self-critical, self-defeating internal cognitions and self-statements that create or amplify personal anxiety.

JOURNAL ENTRY

- Do you experience negative self-statements?
- What has been helpful for you in identifying and modifying problematic internal cognitions?

Addressing Archaic or Infantile Needs

Responsibly tending to self needs is a challenge under the best of circumstances. It is particularly so when some of our needs are "archaic," or incompletely met dependency needs of early childhood, which might include conscious or unconscious wishes to be more appreciated and loved. As therapists, we intellectually tend to agree that archaic or "infantile" needs are not negative per se. Nonetheless, when it comes to our own, we may likely struggle, just as our patients do. We need to remind ourselves, as we do our clients, that these early, primitive needs, even though they may have been originally experienced as "bad" or problematic and subsequently repressed, are nonetheless real and can be very powerful.

A number of writers have spoken on this point. As we know, all humans have "needs of the self for appreciation, attention, and gratification" (Welt & Herron, 1990, p. 308). Yet therapists, as a group, may tend toward "shame and silence about true self needs" (Saakvitne & Pearlman, 1996, p. 41). Goldberg (1991) referred to the stress a therapist experiences when facing "the everyday onslaught of emotional issues without feeling that his/her own emotional needs are being met" (p. 288). Hence, it is critical, Goldberg heeded, for the therapist to become "far more aware than ever before of who he or she is as a persona and of the . . . needs that he or she has, without awareness, yearned to fulfill" (p. 65).

Therapists need to be on the alert for the subtle manifestations of narcissistic needs; Grosch and Olsen (1994) reminded us to "Consider those patients . . . who you especially look forward to seeing or miss when they cancel. . . . Think of the VIP patient who gives you a surge of self-esteem because she elected to see you for her therapy" (p. 40). "Masked narcissism," or tending to others in the service of being appreciated, is a costly dynamic (Grosch & Olsen, 1994).

A. Miller (1981) and Hilton (1997) advocated that therapists come to terms with their primitive psychic wounds and responsibly tend to these wounds, rather than unconsciously depending on the therapist role for comfort and validation. Miller observed,

> The experience of one's own truth, and the postambivalent knowledge of it, makes it possible to return to one's own world of feelings at an adult level—without paradise, but with the ability to mourn. . . . Only after painfully experiencing and accepting our own truth can we be relatively free from the hope that we might still find an understanding, empathic mother—perhaps in a patient— who would be at our disposal. (Miller, 1981, pp. 15, 27)

As a therapist, Hilton (1997) spoke of his own mourning of earlier pain:

> For me to no longer organize my sense of self around the denial of that loss [of receiving good-enough emotional care as a child], I must be able to mourn it. But, that means I accept [the reality of such a loss]. This can be devastating. But, if I have not faced this in my own therapy, I will not be able to let go of this role with my clients. . . . I will be unable to help them let go of the self-destructive roles they have created to avoid experiencing their [own] losses.
> (p. 152)

The critical issue is how we manage archaic needs. Ideally, a mature and adult part of our self can become conscious of and tend to these needs to lessen our risk of indirectly acting them out. We need to develop mature, proactive means of tending to early unmet needs. The challenge is to find ways that are ego syntonic, effective, and maintainable over time.

JOURNAL ENTRY

- What self needs are you aware of that feel old?
- How do you feel about tending to such needs?

Addressing Compulsive Self-Reliance

Compulsive self-reliance (or counterdependence) may be a reaction formation to unmet dependency needs. There is value in becoming more aware of and more appropriately responsive to such needs. We all, as human beings, have dependency needs. The goal is to tend to them rather than risk acting them out, such as in "masked narcissism," which ultimately helps neither the therapist nor the client.

> I've been compulsively self-reliant much of my life. I had to be emotionally independent from my family of origin. That made emotional dependency or emotional needs very frightening. It was alright to be needed, but it wasn't alright to need. (Mahoney, 1997)

JOURNAL ENTRY

- Do you think you're overly self-reliant? If so, how has this dynamic manifested over time?
- How costly has it been for you? How motivated have you been to address this concern?

Transforming Envy

Envious feelings about our colleagues, clients, friends, family, and others are often difficult to tolerate (Frank, 1977; Savlin, 1995; Slakter, 1987). We may feel guilty about envying others even as we are aware of many riches present in our life. In truth, of course, envious feelings are part of the human experience.

Feelings of envy can, in fact, be very useful. They can guide us to better understand what we may need more of in our own life. Hadler (1997) acknowledged her envious feelings stirred in clinical work with an elderly woman and her adult daughter:

> Despite great distance and deep pain, the mother and daughter . . . continued to search for each other . . . a search that led them into therapy. Finally they were able to speak of pain and death. Week after week I saw the two of them break down one wall after another. . . . As the mother faced . . . her life and heard and recognized its effects on her daughter, the relationship with her daughter began to bear fruit. . . . As I listened to them talk, I felt tears in my eyes, longing to hear my mother say those words to me, longing to talk with my mother as two grown women sharing stories about life and death. (p. 34)

We can learn how to take pleasure vicariously in the gifts and achievements of others in our life. Wepman (1997), as a therapist and as a parent, reflected on the transformation of his envious feelings about his sons:

> Not long ago, my sons were beginning to step out into the world, I was feeling depressed, anxious, and resentful. . . . I looked at them—young, handsome men with good abilities and unlimited possibilities, beginning to have success in a world that was just starting to open up to them. I felt envious. I was afraid that my envy would begin to spread its poison into the relationships, but I didn't know what to do. I was having dinner with a friend, and told him what was going on with me. He replied, with a wisdom not unusual for him, how fortunate I was to be a man with enviable sons. With that I felt my perceptions shift. Of course he was right, and I felt that an alchemy had transmuted my envy into admiration. (p. 41)

JOURNAL ENTRY

- ✎ What in your present life rouses envious feelings?
- ✎ Have the stimuli of your envy changed across your life?
- ✎ What clues to your present needs and desires does your envy give you?

Grieving

Loss can occur in many forms. We experience the loss of people, things, time, and opportunities. We also experience loss in relation to our self—loss of self-confidence, loss of self-trust. Grieving for past or present losses is painful, but ultimately relieving.

Few of us necessarily want or choose to go through a grieving process. Yet most of us have hurts to grieve. It's often quite amazing how, without intention, some old, deep, covered-over wound gets bumped, and we find our self once again feeling pain and grief, sometimes to an intense and unexpected degree.

Even if we believe that grieving loss is healthy, we can't just will our self to grieve. We must grant our self the time, space, and support necessary to grieve our losses, which often necessitates the unearthing of entombed pain. Fortunately, when it comes to grieving past losses as adults, we are more likely to have developed the abilities to feel and tolerate the hurt and grief and to be more direct and skillful in tending pain and sadness that may have been intolerable at a younger, more fragile stage. Thus, although the process is not easy, as an adult it is usually tolerable and ultimately cathartic.

JOURNAL ENTRY

- ✎ What has your own experience been with respect to grieving new or old pains?
- ✎ Are you aware of grief you still carry within that is related to past losses?
- ✎ What might be helpful, comforting, or supportive in facilitating a therapeutic grieving process?

Personal Psychotherapy

Certainly, life itself offers opportunity for growth and healing. At the same time, personal therapy for the therapist, be it a beginning or a return, is valuable and empowering for one's self as an individual, personally as well as professionally (Goldberg, 1991; Guy, 1987; Kaslow, 1984; Mahoney, 1998; Norcross, 2000; Pope & Tabachnick, 1994).

Therapy, for the therapist as for others, likely serves different functions at different stages of life. As a young trainee, therapy in the service of deepening self-awareness is invaluable. Granting one's self the option to return to therapy, as a seasoned therapist for further psychotherapy work is also potentially very beneficial, personally and professionally. A more developed ego and deepened life experience contribute to more focused, intensified personal therapy.

> The importance of personal therapy for the therapist cannot be overemphasized, and has been recommended by others as a way of remaining open to ourselves and our clients. . . . It is not only essential, however, as a preparation for the responsible role of therapist, but as a place in which to process the impact and effect of our therapeutic work on ourselves, to take all of our needs, our wishes, our fears, all of our feelings and thoughts. Psychotherapy is a way of understanding and nurturing oneself, a gift one can give oneself, whose benefits also ripple outward to family, friends, clients, and colleagues. (Pearlman & Saakvitne, 1995, p. 394)

Therapy is also an appropriate means of addressing the major occupational hazard of consciously or unconsciously using the demands and involvements of work as a way to avoid dealing with our own personal issues. As Maeder (1989) put it,

> The more difficult, but ultimately more satisfying, road leads to a painful confrontation with [our] own problems and weaknesses, and ultimately to self-knowledge. . . . The end result is a clearer perception of [our] ambitions and needs and their relationship to the task at hand. [The therapist] . . . can approach others with honesty, compassion, and humility, knowing that he is motivated by genuine concern, and not by some ulterior motive. (p. 40)

Hilton (1997) argued for therapy for the therapist in the service of "the actualization of our own being, the integration of body and mind. . . . This recovery means going through all the pain and disappointment of the angst that we felt we could avoid by being psychotherapists" (p. 157).

> My mom . . . raising four kids, not college educated, still a kid herself . . . was able to find the means for me to go see a therapist, and my father paid for it without insurance. That therapy experience was such a big part of my growing up and my education. (Beer, 1997)

Reasons for therapists to be in psychotherapy parallel those experienced by our clients. Freudenberger (1986a) cited "the end of relationships or marriages; feelings of depression, aloneness or loneliness; the attempt or the actual suicide of a patient; and the feelings of failure or rejection in working with patients" (p. 144). Other issues for psychotherapy might include ongoing dissatisfactions, confusion, anxiety, life-stage transitions, fears, constrictions, shame, unrequited personal yearnings, unresolved hurts, or sadness or grief. Therapy can also help us explore options and new choices, address hurts and wounds within our self or between self and others, accept "forbidden feelings" such as envy, hate, or sexual feelings; process traumatic experiences; and incorporate "split off" parts of the self that have been defensively shut down and unprocessed, which may become disruptive if untended.

In general, our needs for seeking therapy, as therapists ourselves, are probably not much different than for most other folks. We take risks, with ourselves and with others, if we neglect our own treatment when appropriate. Psychotherapy both demands ego strength and is ego strengthening. It can be valuable to be on the receiving end of what we offer as therapists ourselves. For some of us, it may be comforting to experience our own therapist as imperfect—but still good enough.

Many therapists acknowledge their doubts about and even reluctance to seek psychological assistance (Kilburg, Nathan, & Thoreson, 1986). A number of esteemed psychologists have offered commentary on this matter:

- It is the unusual therapist . . . who seeks therapeutic intervention for himself or herself comfortably or easily. To many therapists this constitutes "failure." As the physician abhors illness . . . the therapist sees unsureness, self-doubt, and confusion as marks of inadequacy and even a kind of therapist 'sinfulness.' (Kaslow, 1984, p. ix)

- We have been oriented as practitioners—through our training, if not our character—to handle life's most excruciating problems and suffering in private. (Goldberg, 1992, p. 132)

- The use of denial as a coping mechanism may also manifest itself in counterphobic and counterdependent responses. . . . Denial can also be manifested by an unwillingness to seek help for experienced symptoms. . . . To admit need would be to admit dependency on another for aid. This is an especially difficult admission for people who are themselves helpers, and it often serves as a significant deterrent to seeking therapeutic assistance. (Freudenberger, 1986, p. 145)

- Usually the healer–helper has a difficult time viewing himself/herself in the role of patient. He fears a loss of dignity, loss of sense of self, or loss of power; he feels impotent and rather early on voices a loss of self-esteem. He may present himself as masochistic, guilt ridden, feeling ashamed. (Freudenberger, 1986, p. 188)

- There's no question that sometimes practitioners have a blind spot when it comes to needing therapy or consultation for themselves, even when it may be practically important to seek it. We parcel out therapy all day long, but we don't appreciate the need for therapy for ourselves. (Welch, 1999, p. 4)

- Reticence is the biggest roadblock to the professional's pursuit of therapy. Psychologists may hold to an even greater extent than do lay people negative attitudes towards therapy. Although mental health professionals stress the importance of providing services to all persons in need, psychologists and psychiatrists alike exclude one group—their own colleagues. Because of the great emphasis on self-reliance and professional autonomy, there exists an unspoken expectation that healers should need no healing. This tacit standard is reinforced by a parallel and equally unrealistic expectation on the part of patients. Viewing themselves and being viewed by others as paragons of mental health prevent needy psychologists from admitting weakness and seeking help. (Millon, Millon, & Antoni, 1986, p. 131)

- Your own therapy should be a priority in your life. You should have a very clear idea of what it is like to sit on the other side and you should be very clear about what you bring to the equation. . . . The empathy this brings to your work makes you much more attractive to patients. (Lundeen & Geiger, 1999, p. 19)

- Can you give yourself 50 minutes of time every week or two in a holding environment? Are you practicing what you preach regarding the value of psychotherapy? (Guy & Norcross, 1998, p. 390)

> When I have the opportunity to be in the client role with people that I really respect and trust, I don't wait until I've got a big problem, I just cherish the opportunity and go for it.

Mahoney (1997) acknowledged a tendency to wait too long: "Now when I have the opportunity to be in the client role with people that I really respect and trust, I don't wait until I've got a big problem, I just cherish the opportunity and go for it." Clearly, it is hard for many of us to be a patient in therapy. It is difficult to disrupt the status quo and to expose our vulnerability, especially before a colleague we hold in esteem. Under the best of circumstances, it is very sobering to observe and tolerate evidence of our own less than optimally developed psychological functioning and vestiges of primitive defenses. It is all the more difficult for us to seek assistance for problems we deem pathological, correctly or not, out of fear of condemnation.

The therapy process, at various stages, may stir feelings of inadequacy as a person or as a therapist. In the early stage of treatment, the therapist–client's "vulnerability may not be readily accessible. Intrusion into the narcissistic defense system [may be experienced] as an attack that must be repelled at all costs" (Freudenberger, 1984, p. 188). Until trust has been established, we may project judgments onto the treating therapist (for example, "What kind of therapist must she think I am?" "Does he wonder how I can possibly work with all my own primitive baggage and unresolved issues?").

> If I'm too exhausted. . . . I don't have the capacity to even [recognize my exhaustion]. . . . my inner responses don't exist, and that's frightening.

Yet therapy is, in fact, the most appropriate place to address these kinds of issues. In therapy the goal is to be honest and to unburden private, sometimes weighty, issues. The process of being real, and being accepted in our rawness and realness, is powerfully therapeutic for us as well as for our clients. Ideally, the therapist's own psychotherapy is "a sanctuary, a place of such safety and confidentiality that the unthinkable can be thought and discussed" (Blau, 1984, p. ix).

Clearly, the therapist–client must work with a skilled, mature, differentiated therapist. The treating therapist needs to be able both to work collaboratively with the therapist–client on needs and options and to be appropriately confrontational as necessary.

The theoretical orientation of the therapy depends on one's particular concerns and preferences. Experiential therapies, such as psychodrama or dance or art therapy, may help to get below highly developed verbal defenses; therapist–clients are typically cognitively and verbally facile.

Issues of confidentiality and dual relationships are not minor. Even in the largest cities, psychotherapeutic circles can be very close. Concerns that the therapist might discuss one's case in peer supervision with colleagues known professionally or socially should be discussed. Likewise, outside-therapy contact with the treating therapist (for example, at professional or social events) is another matter for forthright discussion.

> One hopes that we can keep the roles separate without becoming so arbitrary that people can't even be in the same room at a professional meeting or social event to which they have both been invited without knowledge that the other would also be in attendance. More attention needs to be paid to where normal, overlapping relationship end and complex, unwise dual relationships begin so that therapists, supervisors, and professors do not find themselves inadvertently and with all good intention violating the above principle. (Kaslow, 1984, p. 32)

JOURNAL ENTRY

✎ Have you been in therapy?
✎ At what stages of your personal and professional development did you enter or re-enter therapy?

◈ Have you wished to seek therapy but had concerns about the process of finding a therapist or of undergoing treatment?

◈ What were these concerns?

◈ What would you like to offer yourself in terms of therapy options at this or perhaps a later time?

Tending Self Physically

It has been said that the body is "the sacred vessel which houses your soul, your authentic self" (Andres, Ebaugh, Feeney, Long, & Zipin, 2001). We rationally know that taking care of our body, as the physical residence of our self, is important. But most of us have a complex relationship with our own body and a range of ambivalent feelings about it. There is immense value in working to accept and make peace with the reality of our physical self as one aspect of our total, fuller self (Burka, 1996; Rabinor, 1995). Dressing comfortably and attractively can be an important aspect of accepting our self physically (Saakvitne & Pearlman, 1996).

We talk with our patients about the essentialness of physical, as well as emotional, self-care. Yet therapists too can neglect of our own physical self needs: "We occasionally become so intent and focused on sophisticated self-care methods that we overlook the basics" (Guy & Norcross, 1998, p. 390).

Modern life has provided immense advantages for physical self-care. For most of us, food is plentifully available; we can eat as much as, or whenever, we want. Electricity allows us to stay up as long as we wish. Automobiles and other modern conveniences minimize the necessity of hard physical activity. At the same time, caring for our self physically requires regular, and regulated, eating, drinking, sleeping, and exercise. For some of us, a casual approach to physical self-care suffices. For others, a proactive regimen of physical health care is necessary to preserve or restore health. Genetic factors influence physical functioning, but our own behavior maximizes or minimizes our genetic blueprint.

JOURNAL ENTRY

◈ How would you describe your relationship with your own body and the care of your body at this stage of your life?

◈ What struggles have continued over time?

◈ What difficulties might you encounter later on?

◈ How comfortable are you with your own body?

✎ Do you feel that you dress in a way that is comfortable for you, personally and professionally? If not, why is that?

✎ When have you felt best, and worst, about your body?

✎ What are your needs, hopes, and goals in this matter?

FOOD AND SUBSTANCE USE

Food and eating are immensely complicated, emotionally charged issues for many of us. Alcohol, tobacco, and other substances are similarly controversial. Even though the self-destructive ingestion of food and other substances is normalized in our own and many other cultures, it entails risks to our physical health and can have a negative impact on our self-esteem. Regulating food intake is essential in maintaining the energy and stamina we need for professional and personal activity and optimizing our health. (A detailed discussion of these topics is beyond the scope of this book; readers can consult the following references for more information: Kesten, 2001; Ornish, 1993; Schneider, 2001; Tallmadge, 2002.)

Moderating food intake is no small task in a culture of plenty. With so much attractive, easily accessible, immensely appealing food, it is very easy to overeat. In addition, in many cultural or social settings, we may feel pressured to eat and drink more, or differently, than is healthy. It is hard to maintain limits when cultural norms or social reactions encourage us to show our heartiness or "big appetite" for life through excessive eating.

Despite the widely known health risks and ineffectiveness of "on-and-off" dieting, it is both fashionable and tempting, albeit irrational, to experiment with the diet of the day. Depriving ourselves of adequate nourishment and then going off the diet, often in a big way, can become reinforcing as a means of self-stimulation, primitive gratification, or diversion or, in some cases, even a dissociative mechanism. Some of us may overwork to divert ourselves from eating too much.

Therapists, as a group, are informed and conscious regarding the benefits of healthful eating and moderate alcohol intake. But as for most human beings, use of food can be emotionally charged and complex issues for many therapists. A literature does exist on therapist substance abuse (Elliott & Guy, 1993; Freudenberger, 1986; Thoreson & Skorina, 1986; O'Connor, 2001), and Rabinor (1995) writes bravely of body image issues as an eating disorders therapist. However, little literature exists in terms of therapists' struggles with food, eating and weight, and how this might affect or be affected by patients with similar problems.

Consciously thinking through some basic guidelines for healthy eating is usually worth the time and effort. For those who have had significant struggles with healthy eating, a consultation with a nutritionist about healthy guidelines for food intake is advisable. Most people gain the following benefits from a well-rounded diet with an appropriate number of calories and moderate exercise:

- a stable blood sugar level;
- weight stabilization;
- a balance between structure and flexibility that is useful alone and or in social settings;
- an antidote to the on-and-off diet roller-coaster;
- a "prosthesis" against using food to act out unprocessed emotional reactions; and
- a long-term habit of monitoring food and other substance intake.

RECREATIONAL SUBSTANCES

Alcohol use, although enjoyable and culturally normative for many of us, is nonetheless a potentially addictive substance. Excessive drinking can seriously compromise our efforts at self-care. Just as with food intake, it is prudent to consciously consider guidelines for alcohol use. The best rule is to drink in a limited, moderate way. If you notice any negative effects from your alcohol use, consider getting more information and to ensure that you prevent further complications.

The health risks associated with tobacco use are virtually irrefutable—for the primary user and for those who are in physical proximity to the user. If you smoke, you can stop—smoking cessation techniques are generally quite effective. Consider getting the assistance of a professional experienced in addictions if you cannot overcome your psychological resistance to quitting.

JOURNAL ENTRY

- How do you feel about your eating as it relates to your self-care?
- How concerned are you about your eating habits?
- How much attention have you given the issue over time?
- What has been most helpful in enabling you to eat in a healthy way?
- How do you feel about the amount you drink and the way you drink?
- Does your drinking seem like an issue to you? to others?
- Do you smoke? If so, have you felt pressure from yourself or from others to stop smoking?

✎ What efforts have you already made to stop smoking?
✎ What has been hard about that process?
✎ What are your hopes and goals for regulating your intake of food and other substances in promoting your self-care?

REST

Physical rest is a basic task in terms of self-care. We need rest to remain healthy. Yet as many of us know, rest can be the first thing we neglect in stressful or especially busy times. Also, we need more rest when we are not feeling well. At the same time, for those in private practice, resting means canceling patients and losing income.

Regular rest is critical to our ability function over the long haul. Without adequate rest, we risk compromised immune functioning and more frequent and chronic colds, body pain, and other physical problems.

The negative effects of sleep deprivation upon mental and physical functioning over time are well documented (Broughton & Olgivie, 1992). Dement (1999), in the course of decades of sleep studies, concludes that approximately half of all Americans "mismanage our sleep to the point where it negatively affects our health and safety" (p. 3). In addition to diminished mental and physical performance and medical problems associated with sleep deprivation, Dement speaks to the more insidious and costly effects of general fatigue and exhaustion and their impact on quality of life. A seasoned therapist observed, "If I'm too exhausted, which I can easily get, I don't have the capacity to even [recognize my exhaustion]. . . . My inner responses don't exist, and that's frightening."

JOURNAL ENTRY

✎ How many hours of sleep do you try to get per night?
✎ Is your sleep schedule regular enough?
✎ How critical is the issue of rest to your own self-care?

EXERCISE

Psychotherapists have sedentary jobs. Because physical inactivity is associated with fatigue, exercise brings mental as well as physical benefits. Sports psychologist Hays (1997) recommended that therapists

> find a type of exercise that is intrinsically pleasing. Choose an exercise that has emotional, as well as physical benefits.

Consider the exercise "FIT," i.e., frequency, intensity or time duration. Recognize the possible sociocultural factors, e.g., gender differences. Consider social support, both helpful and unhelpful. Be aware of external factors that affect, positively or negatively, an on-going exercise program. Establish and review both short-term and longer term goals.

As therapists, most of us are aware of the benefits of exercise. To maintain an ongoing exercise program, it is important to find exercise activities that are fun, energizing, and gratifying. Thirty minutes a day of even moderate activity is enough to help the heart pump blood to the muscles and brain and to burn calories. Sometimes simple exercises—walking, stretching, yoga, swimming, dance, or sports—are the easiest to maintain over time.

JOURNAL ENTRY

- ✎ Do you exercise?
- ✎ What factors help you get regular exercise?
- ✎ If you aren't getting enough regular exercise, what interferes with your exercise goals?
- ✎ How might you overcome these obstacles?

SEXUALITY

As with other issues involving our physical self, the expression and gratification of our sexuality is a complex issue that may vary in intensity and salience over time. Ryff and Singer (1998) spoke sensitively of our need to understand the relationship between our sexuality and our emotional well-being. They speculated

> that those who enjoy loving relationships that are emotionally, sexually, and spiritually fulfilling over long periods of time are those likely to experience better health, both mental and physical. . . . What likely differentiates copulation from making love, and therefore what sets us apart from the beasts, is the degree to which both partners are mentally and physically aroused; the scope of their mutual arousal, and the extent to which the sexual experience enhances their closeness and love, or promotes distance and hostility, or simply disinterest and relief. (p. 75)

Saakvitne and Pearlman (1996), in their recommendations for therapist self care, advise us to "be sexual—with yourself, with a partner" (p. 63).

JOURNAL ENTRY

- ✎ Does your journal feel safe and private enough to note some of your honest feelings on sexuality?

✎ What feels positive to you in terms of your sexuality?
✎ What do you see as areas of concern or challenge?

MEDICAL CARE

To adequately care for our self physically, we must be responsible about getting routine medical care. It is important to find and develop a good collaborative relationship with a personal physician, a dentist, and other health professionals as needed. We need to schedule an annual physical exam and regular dental cleaning. We also need to comply with medication prescriptions, including psychotropic medication if appropriate: "Some of us need to confront our ambivalence about medication. Many therapists who are quite skillful at persuading their clients to try antidepressants are ashamed of their own use of Prozac" (Treadway, 1998, p. 60). Holistic and alternative treatments, such as acupuncture, may also be valuable aspects of medical care.

JOURNAL ENTRY

✎ How do you evaluate yourself in terms of your medical care?
✎ Is there anything, psychologically or otherwise, that interferes with your developing a team of health caregivers to tend to you as needed?

Tending Self Spiritually

Although psychology early on recognized the importance of the spirit, as well as of the mind and body (W. R. Miller, 1999), only recently has spirituality been discussed at any length in contemporary psychology. Starr and Weiner (2000) listed three usages of the term *spirituality:*

1. in "a humanistic sense—caring for the planet and environment, empathy for and acceptance of diversity, giving service to communities and the needy, and other selfless activities";
2. "as comprehensive philosophies and principles that emanate from the great world religions"; and
3. as distinct from formalized, ritualized religion per se, with "spirituality focusing more on the nature of the spiritual self and its relationship to divinity or a higher 'something'" (p. 4).

Principles or elements associated with spirituality include uncertainty, or the impossibility of fully knowing or understanding everything in life, faith, mystery, meaningfulness, connectedness, higher consciousness, gratitude, compassion, forgiveness, universality, surrender, suffering, and redemption (Starr & Weiner, 2000, pp. 7–10).

Any combination of forces, including age and experience, may drive us to search for other, deeper forms of meaning over time. Many of us feel a need to focus on something beyond worldly pains and gratifications:

> We have to find a way to connect our small, insignificant lives to a pattern of purpose and meaning in the universe in whatever way we understand it. This sense of being allows us to soldier forth every day knowing that being responsive to our clients' suffering can make a difference, and that we are not responsible for their lives. (Treadway, 1998, p. 61)

> I found that things I initially thought were going to be satisfying to the self, like getting a massage or going out for a lovely lunch by myself near the ocean, that while those kinds of things are really deeply satisfying, that the self wants something deeper than that. It's a longing at a much deeper level. Such activities may provide relief, or interruption, or physical activity may give a certain energy or high. But as human beings, we're looking for something more. And that's the miracle of being human, because there is something greater and deeper to be gotten. . . . I think people become therapists because they're searching for deeper answers. They're asking big life questions. (Riskin, 1997)

> I think people become therapists because they're searching for deeper answers. They're asking big life questions

ASSOCIATION BETWEEN SPIRITUALITY AND WELL-BEING

Empirical data tend to support the myriad personal testimonies about the relationship between spirituality and psychological and physical well-being (W. R. Miller, 1999). Clinical research has observed the effects of prayer, contemplation, meditation, yoga, and ritual in reducing medical symptoms and improving medical recoveries (Emmett, 1999; Pargament, 1997). A renowned researcher of mind–body practices, Herbert Benson (1996), speculated that spiritual experience serves as a physical balm to counter the rapid pulse and adrenaline rush associated with stress. Other research reveals a relationship between elements of spirituality (for example, connection with others and self, sense of meaning and purpose in life, hopefulness and optimism) and higher levels of psychological functioning (W. R. Miller, 1999).

JOURNAL ENTRY

✎ Does the association between spirituality and well-being make sense to you?

✎ Have you seen examples of this association or experienced it personally?

✎ Is spirituality a facet, directly or indirectly, of your work as a therapist?

SPIRITUAL PRACTICES

Spiritual practices range from involvement in traditional, formal, organized religion to more eclectic, informal, individualized versions. Many of us grew up with the former to a greater or lesser extent, but we can also benefit from the latter in caring for our self in a holistic way. Zeiss (1997) spoke of the importance of being

> part of something infinite. We're not a religious family. . . . We don't go to church . . . [but] there's a particular place . . . a waterfall in the Santa Cruz mountains. . . . It's always there, and it's very beautiful. . . . If I lose my connection to that, I would lose my power in a sense. It's what sustains me.

"Mind–body practices" can deepen and facilitate our emotional, mental, and physical awareness and harmony. Meditation is one of the best-known forms of mind–body practice. Yoga, tai chi, self-hypnosis, guided imagery, therapeutic massage, biofeedback, visualization, stretching, deep muscle relaxation, and breathing exercises are other forms of mind–body practices.

Meditation "is really about making the time to experience your own essence" (Rabinor & Kearney-Cooke, 1998, p. 3). There are many versions of meditation. The widely-used Benson (1975) approach involves sitting quietly; concentrating intently on some object, sound, or word or on one's breathing; visualizing a pleasant scene; and then breathing deeply, consciously relaxing the body and mind. "Mindfulness meditation" draws from Buddhist tradition and involves intentionally focusing one's attention on the present moment, without judging or reacting (Kabat-Zinn, 1994; Wittine, 1995): "Mindfulness means paying attention in a particular way, on purpose, in the present moment, and nonjudgmentally. This kind of attention nurtures greater awareness, clarity and acceptance of present-moment reality" (Kabat-Zinn, 1994, p. 4).

Journal writing can be used in developing spiritual self-care. Christina Baldwin (1991) described her journal as her "life's companion. . . . It urges me to remember to pay attention to spirit" (p. 11). She noted,

There's a particular place . . . a waterfall in the Santa Cruz mountains. . . . it's always there, and it's very beautiful. . . . if I lose my connection to that, I would lose my power in a sense. It's what sustains me.

Spiritual writing expands the interior conversation of consciousness to include your relationship with the sacred. You are no longer alone on the quest, or on paper. You are in conversation with Something you perceive as beyond, or deep within, yourself. It is this inclusion of the sacred that spiritualizes the writing. (Baldwin, 1991, p. 23)

Retreats are another potentially spiritual practice. A retreat to a quiet, serene setting, be it for a day, a weekend, or longer, offers us the opportunity to gain perspective, deal with life events, reflect on personal goals, grow spiritually, and deepen our sense of connection with our own existence and with the universe (Rehnke, 1997). Retreats offer us time and opportunity to read, to write in our journal, to pray or meditate, and to enjoy nature (Cooper, 1999):

> Outdoor recreation refills my depleted spiritual resources best of all. Hiking alone in the nearby mountains . . . kayaking out on the ocean . . . that does a lot for my spirit.

The time I spend alone is probably the most spiritual. The time I spend thinking and reflecting and contemplating, or just simply praying does a lot to keep me in touch with my soul. Outdoor recreation refills my depleted spiritual resources best of all. Hiking alone in the nearby mountains . . . kayaking out on the ocean . . . that does a lot for my spirit. I value my spiritual side and I know that it refreshes my work. So I'm pretty deliberate and intentional about what I do to take care of that spiritual side. I've found it to be one of the most valuable resources I have in coping with the stress and isolation of the work I do. (Guy, 1996, p. 6)

Established retreat facilities can offer a retreat on an individual basis or as part of a group program. A number of available publications describe retreat settings around the country (Baji-Holms, 1999; Lederman, 1998).

My involvement with [a women's support group connected with a] Quaker meeting has been helpful, just even the quiet. It feels like a supportive presence of others. . . . Some time outside of work . . . the centering . . . that's been very helpful to me (Callahan, 1996).

JOURNAL ENTRY

- ✎ How do you feel about your own spiritual practices?
- ✎ Have they changed over time?
- ✎ Are there any ways you might wish to grow and develop spiritually?

Professional Challenges 5

As most of us already know, we work in a field which can be exceedingly gratifying, excruciatingly demanding, certainly frustrating, and, at moments, truly frightening . . . Based on the nature of our discipline, we also deal with particular pressures and risks. (Baker, 1984, p. 1)

The rewards of our work are potentially rich and plentiful, both psychologically and spiritually (Radeke & Mahoney, 2000). We learn an immense amount about human nature, and about our own self, in the process. Being present with our patients exercises our capacity to be present and grounded in our own self. In helping others, we offer ourselves the same transformative opportunity (Rabinor, 1999). Truly, the subject of the therapeutic benefits of being a therapist is worthy of a book in itself.

Nonetheless, the reality is that the rewards of the work are intertwined with significant responsibilities and stresses, and with "complex demands, human costs, constant risks, and often limited resources" (Pope & Vasquez, 1998, p. 1). This chapter provides an overview of the inherent professional concerns and contemporary pressures associated with working as a psychologist. Being conscious of the risks our work involves may stir a degree of anxiety, when we stop to think about it. Yet, for many of us, it may be validating and reassuring to remember that we share concerns with both our colleagues and our fellow human beings.

JOURNAL ENTRY

✎ As you anticipate reviewing the professional demands and pressures you face, what thoughts and feelings come to mind?

99

Concerns Inherent in Providing Psychotherapy

THERAPY-CENTERED DEMANDS

Complexity, Inexactness, and Gradualness

Indisputably, psychotherapy is a complicated, inexact, and relatively slow process. The work involves both science and artistry, however inexact. We attempt to understand an incredibly complex interplay of multiple human systems and simultaneously to deal with the complexity and subtleties of the therapist–patient interaction. Growth and change for our clients, as for the rest of us, usually occurs in small increments: "Our work goes on behind closed doors, sometimes for years. The goals are individual. Success or failure is not easily measured" (Ablow, 1992, p. 100).

JOURNAL ENTRY

- How do you feel about the complexity and inexactness of working as a therapist?
- How stressful or bothersome is that for you?
- How have your views on this matter changed over time?

Potency and Limits of Psychotherapy

Accumulating empirical evidence demonstrates the potency and effectiveness of psychotherapy. Clinical research indicates that a significant portion of patients benefit substantially from psychotherapy (Seligman & Csikszentmihalyi, 2000). Recent neurobiological studies indicate evidence of experience-related "plastic" changes in the human nervous system over the lifespan. Psychotherapy, like psychotropic medication, appears to have the potential, in some cases, to modify brain structure and function, as now measurable by sophisticated modern brain-imaging technology (Vaughan, 1998).

At the same time, as any seasoned psychotherapist knows, there are limits in terms of what we can know and understand about the client's inner experience and what we can accomplish in our clinical work. There are also limits to the degree that we can help our patients. It is impossible to anticipate how much can be accomplished in psychotherapy or how quickly—or slowly—the work will proceed.

So many factors influence the speed and intensity of the psychotherapeutic progress. Those of us working in a managed care environment must accomplish treatment in a circumscribed number of sessions. Likewise, we usually have minimal influence over the client's environment. Ultimately, we are forced to realize that not everyone can be helped—a painful, but undeniable, reality.

JOURNAL ENTRY

✎ What have your learned, both personally and professionally, about the potency and limits of psychotherapy?

Time- and Labor-Intensive Work

For therapists, time is our ultimate commodity. Not only is it a key raw material for our product; "time is money, particularly in a fee-for-service environment" (Bloch, 1986, p. ix). We did not choose work that is particularly expedient or efficient, as defined in industrial terms. Therapy is time- and labor-intensive work; our work demands our physical, and well as psychological, presence. The reality is that "independent practice does not provide for sick days . . . personal days . . . nor does independent practice provide for paid vacations" (Freudenberger & Kurtz, 1990, p. 468). Taking time off from work may result not only in loss of income, but potentially in loss of patients.

JOURNAL ENTRY

✎ How do you feel about the time and labor intensiveness of your work as a psychotherapist?
✎ How much does it bother you?
✎ How well do you feel you are balancing work and time off from work?

Ethical Responsibilities

As therapists, we deal with two general ethical responsibilities: (a) to provide the best patient care possible; and (b) to maintain our own well-being in the service of optimal patient care. The American Psychological Association (APA, 1992) *Ethical Principles of Psychologists and Code of Conduct*, which is currently under revision, is divided into a preamble, six general principles (which are aspirational rather than necessarily enforceable), and an operational code of conduct. The APA Ethics Code "has as its primary goal the welfare and protection of the individuals and groups with whom psychologists work" (p. 3). APA members are bound to abide by the Ethics code, and even nonmember psychologists and students must uphold its tenets or face possible sanctions. In addition, psychologists are responsible for knowing and adhering to their respective state licensure codes.

Managing and protecting confidential information (Jeffords, 1999; Montgomery, Cupit, & Wimberley, 1999; Shuman & Foote, 1999) is a basic tenet of psychological ethics and is also a hallmark of good therapist–client boundaries. Nonetheless, 62% of clinicians surveyed (Pope & Vasquez, 1998) self-reported that they had unintentionally disclosed confidential information. It is imperative that we disclose privileged patient information only under the conditions set forth in the Ethics Code. We must be constantly on guard against breaching patient confidentiality when it might feel tempting, relieving, or ego-boosting.

JOURNAL ENTRY

✎ Have ethical questions arisen in your work as a therapist?
✎ Have you ever had concerns or experienced anxiety about the ethics of something you or a colleague did in the practice of psychology?
✎ Do you believe you handled the matter proactively or not?
✎ Have you ever felt that patient confidentiality was being breached, by yourself or by a colleague?
✎ What measures do you take to preserve your patients' right to confidentiality?
✎ Do you see therapist self-care as an ethical issue?

Boundary Issues

It is the involvement with the very depths of the being of an individual that makes our role so different.

Boundaries refers to the figurative lines that delineate each of us as separate, unique beings. Good boundaries allow us both to be considerate of ourselves and to connect with others appropriately. Most of us struggle, from time to time, to find and maintain the subtle but immensely important distinction between being connected and blurring the boundary between our self and our patients. It is no small feat to be emotionally attuned to what is going on with a patient and to simultaneously maintain connection with self, to be aware and understanding of our own inner response. The therapeutic and ethical responsibilities of clinical work necessitate both that we practice and model differentiation between our own and our patient's feelings and that we switch back and forth between our emotional connection with the patient and our own intellectual resources to make rational sense of the emotional dynamics we are perceiving.

Maintaining good therapist–client boundaries is a major part of both patient care and therapist self-care (Barnett, 1996; Barnett & Sarnel, 2000; Gabbard & Lester, 1996; Heath, 1991; Peterson, 1992; Sussman, 1992; Welch, 1999; Welt & Herron, 1990). Appropriate therapist–client boundaries

> allow a psychological distance between the therapist and the patient without loss of empathy. They prevent the therapist from being overwhelmed by the patient's . . . symptomatology and allow the therapist to use his or her own fantasies and feelings about the patient, which are reactions to the patient or the patient's projections. (Heath, 1991, p. 9)

Clear, explicit therapist–client policy statements can help us articulate therapist–client boundaries. Such statements are written policies regarding session length, financial arrangements, appointment cancellation policy, and telephone contact that can be given to patients at the start of therapy.

> Within the limits of that 45 minute session . . . we talk about everything and anything that might come up between us. But it's very clear that we act on none of that outside of that frame. (Frank, 1997)

It is the responsibility of the therapist to maintain good therapist–client boundaries. Barnett (1996) observed that "consideration of patient needs and interests is of vital importance when making decisions on boundary issues and dual relationships. . . . Keep the patient's needs paramount" (p. 139). Clients with a high sensitivity to rejection, such as those with personality disorders and narcissistic vulnerabilities, are all the more in need of solid therapeutic boundaries. Boundary infractions may recreate family of origin dysfunction and may result in neglectful treatment and possible iatrogenic effects (therapy-induced harm).

Maintaining appropriate boundaries in out-of-session contact with current or former clients is important as well. Unanticipated contact can feel odd and provoke anxiety for both client and therapist. It is sometimes difficult to know what and how much to say, particularly if spouses or others are present. It is up to the therapist to guide the encounter by saying enough to ease the situation and still respect the boundaries of the therapist–client relationship.

With experience and practice we learn how to identify and navigate our way through the subtle dynamics of maintaining appropriate boundaries, but even seasoned therapists can be vulnerable to boundary loss under enough stress. According to Schoener and Gonsiorek (1988), the risk is that "professional boundaries break down as intimacy grows, and there is excessive therapist self-disclosure, seductive game-playing, excessive use of touch, and social or business involvements outside" therapy sessions (p. 228).

Sometimes we must acknowledge that we feel a special affinity toward a certain patient; such feelings entail the risk of boundary loss. Barnett (1996) admonished, "Keep alert to the way you interact with patients and for warning signs of boundary violations. Are you treating one patient differently than most others; thinking or feeling differently about this patient than most others?" (pp. 138–139). We need to learn how to make use of, and thereby contain, beyond-session thoughts about patients (Kramen-Kahn & Hansen, 1998). Guy and Norcross (1998) recommended, "Identify the client who provides you with the greatest amount of nurturance. How does this make you feel? How are you handling this?" (p. 389).

Working as a therapist inherently entails the experience of "predictable erotic, voyeuristic, and sexual feelings" (Pearlman & Saakvitne, 1995, p. 370). Many of us, at some point, feel sexually attracted to a certain client (Pope, Sonne, & Holroyd, 1993). As antithetical to ethical practice as these feelings may be, they are nonetheless very human. The emotional intimacy of the therapy setting is not unlike that associated with romantic intimacy. A client, or a therapist, who is emotionally vulnerable may develop a romanticized attachment to the other:

> Whenever two people come into proximity with each other, a greater or lesser degree of sexual energy is generated. . . . It is stronger in some instances than in others, but it is always there. People choose, however, to express it in different ways. . . . The client . . . tends to be in an emotionally vulnerable position, expressing needs for closeness, caring, nurturance, and love which may be experienced as indistinguishable from sexual desire. . . . Sometimes the therapist also is vulnerable, with unresolved personal problems and discontents that spill over (consciously or otherwise) into the professional hour. Over a period of time these two people develop a . . . kind of intimacy often . . . associated with sexual intimacy; it is not surprising, then, that people make the same association in therapy. (Edelwich, 1982, p. xvi)

Our responsibility is to observe and manage these feelings and to refuse to act on them. Peer support, supervision, or personal therapy are appropriate means of exploring what is going on psychodynamically in a therapist with feelings of sexual attraction toward a patient. Pope et al. (1993) offered guidance to therapists in clarifying dynamics and considering options when managing sexual responses experienced in the context of a therapeutic relationship.

Bryant Welch (1999), a psychologist and attorney involved in professional liability and risk management, spoke to the correlation between unmet personal needs and risk of boundary violation:

> Although exploitative therapists certainly exist, the personally deprived psychologist is much more prevalent in boundary violation cases. Something is missing—a loved one is lost, or there's a personal problem or feeling of inadequacy. The therapist may feel isolated and vulnerable. When we are personally deprived, we are much more vulnerable to the pull of a patient. The patients' wishes for a more intimate relationship become the therapist's wishes. That's a problem! (p. 3)

Clearly, our challenge is to be aware of and responsible for our own self needs and to recognize our needs as separate and distinct from the needs of our clients. The therapy contract is for "sufficient self–object differentiation . . . so the relationship can indeed be a relationship, not a quasi-two person experience whereby one person is an extension of the other or in the emotional service of the other" (Welt & Herron, 1990, p. 5). Guy and Norcross (1998) stated it bluntly, "Your clients are not there to meet your needs: treatment relationships are not reciprocal" (p. 389). Barnett (1996) advised the following:

> Be sensitive to factors which leave you vulnerable to boundary violations—issues of impairment or distress such as substance abuse, personal problems, or ongoing stresses in your life. Be prepared to limit your scope of practice, obtain consultation or supervision, and possibly seek treatment for yourself. (p. 139)

JOURNAL ENTRY

- How do you assess your ability to manage boundaries appropriately with your clients?
- What would threaten or undermine to your ability to maintain appropriate therapist–patient boundaries?
- What do you do to protect against such vulnerabilities?
- Has stage of personal and professional development affected your ability to hold boundaries with patients? In what ways?
- Do you have a policy statement? If not, is this something you've thought about implementing?
- Is there someone you would feel safe with in talking about any concerns about clinical boundaries?
- Have you experienced feelings of sexual attraction to a client?
- What has been helpful for you in working through such feelings?

CLIENT-CENTERED OBLIGATIONS

Our clients' needs are boundless and complex. Even if we are able to work with a chosen clientele, some clients are more difficult to work with than others because of the extent of their problems and needs and the challenges of their interpersonal dynamics. Regardless of theoretical orientation, our work involves empathically being with clients' deep pain and ellusive, unarticulated "primitive material." All clients are in need of feedback and mirroring in some form.

The way our clients relate to us, particularly under stress, helps us better understand their internal dynamics and their interactions with significant others. Nevertheless, it can be grueling and challenging to "deal constructively with patients' hostility, negativism, provocations, and other resistances that are part and parcel of the difficulties that bring them to therapy and that are regularly enacted in therapy" (Strupp, 1996, p. 1017).

Our caseloads often include clients with a phenomenal range of acute and chronic problems, including anxiety and panic, depression, along with life-and-death issues. A significant portion of our clientele are bruised, fragile, vulnerable, helpless, dependent, resistant, untrusting, immaturely defended, highly reactive, traumatized, and personality disordered. Many are narcissistic, impulsive, demanding, entitled, disdainful, harsh, critical, intimidating, manipulative, exploitative, passive–aggressive, hostile, intimidating. Some are even aggressive, threatening, or potentially capable of harming or killing self or someone else. A few are potentially litigious or interminable.

For most therapists, only a relatively few clients take a disproportionate amount of energy. Not surprisingly, those cases cause an equally disproportionate amount of anxiety. Pope (Div. 42 listserv, February 25, 1999) reported findings from his 1993 study with Tabachnick of a national study of therapists that found that "about 97% reported fear that a client would commit suicide, about 83% that a client would physically attack them, and about 89% that a client would attack a third party. Over a fourth (about 29%) reported that a client had committed suicide; about 19% reported that a client had physically attacked them; and about 61% reported that a client had physically attacked a third party."

The size and composition of our caseloads likely corresponds with our professional and personal developmental stage, personality, financial needs, and ongoing life events. Experience teaches us how best to schedule the workday to accommodate our caseload. We need to pay attention to, and adjust accordingly, the number of clinical hours we can handle each day and week, keeping in mind how early we like to begin in the morning and how late we prefer to work in the day. Building in breaks for lunch and breathing time between clients is key to optimal scheduling. Kramen-Kahn and Hansen (1998) advised incorporating in simple and brief self-comforting activities over the course of the day and between sessions, regularly and as needed, such as water or tea breaks. A seasoned therapist shared the following:

> There was a period when I was going through so much grief about losing various members of my family, it was absolutely clear to me, I could not deal with people whose issues were so similar. I was young professionally, at the time, but it helped me appreciate and know what it feels like when something is too close to me. It's what I would call a lesson learned the hard way.

JOURNAL ENTRY

- What kinds of clients do you most, and least, prefer to work with?
- What percentage of your practice is of the former? of the latter?
- How much stress and drain do you experience in working with the latter group?
- What is a realistic guideline for you at this stage in terms of how many demanding, complicated cases you can deal with at a time?
- What client concerns seem too close to you own to allow you the clarity and perspective you need to best function professionally?
- How do you feel about your current schedule?
- Are there any particular changes you would like to make in the near future? Perhaps later on?

As psychotherapists, we have a clinical contract with our patients, be it explicit or implicit. Essentially, that contract includes both aspirations and goals as well as specific guidelines about the therapeutic process.

JOURNAL ENTRY

- In your own language, what is your clinical contract?
- How do think you are upholding this contract as you define it?
- In what ways are you satisfied and not satisfied with it?
- Has your conceptualization and understanding of your clinical contract changed over time? In what ways?

Standards of Care

Standards of care pertain to the two major areas of clinical services, assessment and intervention. As stated in the *Ethical Principles of Psychologists and Code of Conduct* (APA, 1992) in section 1.05, Maintaining Expertise, practicing psychologists are responsible for maintaining "a reasonable level of awareness of current scientific and professional information in their fields of activity and undertake ongoing efforts to maintain competence in the skills they use" (p. 4).

Barnett (1996) noted, "Be aware of the relevant standards of care and expectations within your clinical setting and area of specialization. Deviations from the standard of care, even if small at first, may signal blurred boundaries and a progressive potential for exploitation or harm" (p. 139). The effect of the therapist is as important as therapist intent.

JOURNAL ENTRY

- ✎ How well do you feel you uphold appropriate standards of care with your patients?
- ✎ Have you ever felt that you were deviating from those standards?
- ✎ Were you conscious of a sense of choice at the time?
- ✎ In retrospect, would you repeat your choice or choices again or not?

THERAPIST-CENTERED PRESSURES

Physical and Emotional Demands

Undertaking the role of psychotherapist entails the heavy responsibility of being emotionally and psychologically able and strong. Much of the time we bear this responsibility well. The challenge is how to ensure that we can continually meet the physical and emotional demands of practicing psychotherapy. For starters, we need, as therapists, to be in good psychological, physical, and spiritual condition. We need to care for our self in all the ways described in chapter 4.

> The preparation takes energy itself throughout the day and between session, between contacts with people. Whether it's at night, or in the morning, we're conscious that we're going to need to be in good shape to do that. So we prepare. We don't want to overeat . . . or we don't want to not get enough sleep, or if something upsets us between

sessions, we want to get it resolved before the next person comes in, or at least store it some place for then. (Goldstone, 1996)

Personal Involvement

Relational and intersubjective views of therapy argue that "the therapist is always involved, whether or not his or her involvement is expressed directly" (Celenza, 1998, p. 393). Changes and effects occur in both directions, within both client and therapist (Goldfried, 2001; Guy, 1987; Kahn & Fromm, 2001). Psychotherapist-writer Kenneth Ablow (1992) spoke of the therapist–client relationship:

> I know that we are connected, one to another, in complex, perhaps inexplicable, ways we know precious little about. (p. xvi) . . . The work ensnares us. With all the attention to maintaining the structure of the therapeutic relationship, all the emphasis on the symbolic importance of money changing hands, all the limits on disclosing our personal lives, we sometimes grow to love our patients. (p. 101)

Yalom (1989) poignantly acknowledged that, in truth,

> Patienthood is ubiquitous; the assumption of the label is largely arbitrary and often more dependent on cultural, educational, and economic factors than on the severity of pathology. . . . We psychotherapists simply cannot cluck with sympathy and exhort patients to struggle resolutely with their problems. Instead . . . our life, our existence, will always be riveted to death, love to loss, freedom to fear, and growth to separation. We are, all of us, in this together. (p. 14)

JOURNAL ENTRY

- ✎ How have you been personally affected by your work? Positively? Negatively or problematically?
- ✎ How much is the latter a current concern?
- ✎ What has been helpful in resolving the negative effects of doing therapy?

Emotional Control

Whatever the therapist's theoretical orientation, a degree of "restraint and abstinence" is necessary to maintain perspective in the service of insight and understanding (Guy, 1987). We must be prepared to manage, contain, and modulate our internal emotional reactions in sessions with clients or other charged, provoc-

> I went in with the idealistic notion of "I'm going to serve other people" . . . really without anticipating that the process was going to really impact and accelerate my own development . . . sometimes in ways and rates that I did not want. . . .

ative situations. Some of these reactions can be intense and powerful and may include angry, aggressive, or sexual feelings. In addition, therapists have the challenge of containing feelings from one session to another to minimize carryover or "bleeding" of strong feelings from one patient to another. We also need to manage any out-of-session discomfort or anxiety related to an upcoming or previous session.

JOURNAL ENTRY

✎ How well do you feel you contain your emotions within and between sessions?
✎ Has this ability developed with age and experience?
✎ Are there ways you would still like to grow?
✎ Are there situations in which you might be less in charge of your emotions?
✎ What resources do you have to process these situations?

Self as Instrument

Our use of our own personal sensibilities and vulnerabilities in the therapeutic process—the notion of the self as instrument—can contribute greatly to the quality of our work but requires enormous effort to manage. There is a direct relationship between psychological vulnerabilities and the potential for therapeutic sensitivity (Winnicott, 1965). Goldberg (1991) observed,

> The practitioner must remain vulnerable and, at the same time, professional and skillful. We must be openly human, which means being less than the ideal for which we strive, without regarding our limitations as weaknesses or our efforts as failures. . . . Our vulnerabilities are the bridges to our clients. (p. 364)

Our vulnerabilities are the bridges to our clients.

Shellenberger (1997) spoke of the need to be on guard against the hazards of using her own personal experience with a serious illness in her clinical work. She described her goal as being

> to enhance the quality of the therapy through empathy without compromising it by overidentification. I consulted with colleagues who could help me see my blind spots. Additionally, I kept my personal and professional support systems close, got substantial rest, managed my stress level, and stayed focused on my own physical and emotional recovery. (p. 240)

JOURNAL ENTRY

✎ What is your own experience in using your self as an instrument in the therapeutic process?

✎ Are you conscious of using your human emotional experience in the process of connecting and relating with your clients?

✎ What kinds of clients are you more likely to experience deeper empathy or connection with?

✎ Have you ever been concerned about feeling "too much" empathy, or vulnerability, with particular clients?

The "Good-Enough" Therapist

> [There is] conflict between the feeling that you want to be there as the nurturer and [yet] there's only so much that you're capable of giving. . . . I can feel conflict in terms of guilt and a sense of selfishness when I draw the line.

Welt and Herron (1990) spoke of the goal of being a "good-enough" therapist. The term "good enough" was borrowed from Winnicott (1965), who referred to the "good enough" mother who meets the infant's needs both well and consistently enough so that the infant thrives not only physically but also emotionally.

In the profession of psychotherapy, as in most professions, there is a fine line between being competent enough and being perfect. The former is a reasonable goal; the latter is impossible. Our perspective on this issue can significantly affect the degree of pressure we experience at work and the therapy process. If we believe that the therapist and client are collaborators working together to further understand the client's feelings, needs, and options in caring for self, this collaboration will likely be satisfying for both therapist and client. In effect therapy is a place where the client can "be in relation" with his or her self and with the therapist. If, on the other hand, we believe that the therapist must be the all-knowing authority, we will inevitable fail to meet our unreasonable expectations for our own performance and leave the client entrenched in the dependent role.

Acknowledging the value of the process of therapy and remaining conscious of our limits as therapists can help us accept our own good-enough performance. Many or us find deep satisfaction in the "exercise of skills, the human contact, the emotional involvement, the development of a rapport and a dialogue with clients, and the pleasure of doing an important job well" (Edelwich, 1980, p. 217). The reality is that progress, and sometimes significant change, can and does occur for many of our clients, albeit usually in small steps. Frank (1997) spoke of the

> conflict between the feeling that you want to be there as the nurturer and [yet] there's only so much that you're capable of giving. . . . I can feel conflict in terms of guilt and

a sense of selfishness when I draw the line. I wish I didn't feel quite as conflicted about that as I do. There are therapists who don't.

> **I believe that mistakes in therapy are often opportunities for learning.**

Psychotherapy, like all professions, has a learning curve. Ours is sometimes at the expense, usually minor but sometimes more significant, of the client. This is a painful possibility to tolerate. The reality is that clinical errors happen. To ensure that the therapy we provide is good enough, we must responsibly assess the severity of any mistakes and respond to them as proactively as possible. Depending on the severity of the error, we may need to seek supervision from a trusted, respected colleagues. Our ultimate goal is to genuinely try to learn from such experience and, just as importantly, to forgive ourselves. "Jim Bugental and his work on authenticity has really been helpful to me. I believe that mistakes in therapy are often opportunities for learning," (Mahoney, 1997).

JOURNAL ENTRY

- ✎ How would you define a "good-enough" therapist?
- ✎ How do you assess yourself in these terms?
- ✎ How do you feel about your limits in terms of how much you can appropriately give your patients?
- ✎ Do you feel you're able to be a good-enough therapist and still balance your other needs and interests?

Therapeutic Judgment

As practitioners, we are trained to base our professional judgment and interventions on "the evolving theoretical and empirical knowledge and experiences of the discipline" (APA, 1992). Given the complex nature of our work, we are required to make ongoing judgment calls as to what, when, and how much to say or do. Each judgment call involves a certain level of risk and responsibility. The appropriateness and timing of personal disclosure is one such example. We also make judgment calls when we are pressured to provide short-term relief of symptoms without having the time to fully understand the highly complex dynamics underlying those symptoms.

Likewise, our work also involves judgment about when to use confrontation:

> Confrontation takes a heavy toll on the therapist as well as on the client. . . . We are paid specifically to say things to the client that nobody else has the courage and finesse to say. By giving the client honest feedback regarding his

behavior, we take the risk that he will be unwilling or unable to deal with the reality of his situation. . . . The therapist is thus saddled with the responsibility of judging just when calculated risks may be taken, when the client can best handle the painful truth. (Kottler, 1993, p. 20)

We must also make judgment calls about the appropriateness a timing of referring the client or terminating treatment.

JOURNAL ENTRY

✎ How do you feel about the responsibilities inherent in the judg ment calls you make as a therapist?

✎ How do you view your ability to make the most therapeuti judgment calls with your patients?

Therapist Idealization and Role Demand

Potency is attributed to us in our role as a therapist. Our clie view us as a source of information, enrichment, and protecti "In any psychotherapist . . . an unusual degree of self-assuranc essential. . . . Patients force therapists into a position of superio through their idealization" (Maeder, 1989, p. 44). As psychoth apists, we have considerable influence over at least some aspe of our patient's lives. Clients often become vulnerable in the cou of therapy, and the therapist's word and sanction can mean a gr deal.

Outside the therapeutic context, benign occurrences of ide zation are ubiquitous. At social gatherings, we may be asked opinion "as a therapist," or we may be told "thanks for listenin as if our thoughts or presence is more valuable as a psycholog Although the idealization may be flattering at times, it may a seem burdensome, or unjustified. Goldberg (1991) spoke to

the strain of being an idealized person . . . when the practitioner experiences him/herself as merely human—all too human. For no matter how intelligent, well-trained, experienced, caring, and well-meaning we are as professionals, we are, at the same time host to the same fears, ambitions, and temptations. (p. 364)

JOURNAL ENTRY

✎ How do you feel when someone idealizes you as a therapist?
✎ Does the idealization feel flattering or burdensome?
✎ How concerned are you about this matter at this time?
✎ Has it been more problematic for you at certain stages in you career than others?

> Confrontation takes a heavy toll on the therapist as well as on the client. . . . we are paid specifically to say things to the client that nobody else has the courage and finesse to say.

Psychic Isolation

Psychic isolation is a risk inherent in the practice of psychotherapy. For many of us, much of our work is done in a closed room with only one other person present. When we're not seeing patients, we may still be alone in our office. We are also limited in how far we can go from our office between sessions, in part because we are "tied to the clock" (Guy, 1987, p. 83).

Stress caused by external events, such as the encroachment of managed care, or personal issues can also cause us to feel alone. We may be tempted to presume that we are alone or the exception, that others must be handling such matters better.

JOURNAL ENTRY

- Have you felt physically or psychologically isolated at times? If so, in what ways?
- What kinds of symptoms or problems have manifested?
- What has been helpful in addressing these feelings?
- If isolation remains a problem, what options might you further explore?

Countertransference

Therapists experience a vast range of feelings in the context of their work. Some of the most unsettling include frustration, anger, irritation, resentment, pain, shame, fear, sexual attraction, anxiety, confusion, inadequacy, exposure, self-doubt, and need for reassurance and comfort. In a national survey of psychologists, Pope and Tabachnick (1993) found that over 80% of the respondents reported experiencing such feelings.

Freud considered the therapist's response to the client, or countertransference, an impediment to therapy (Slakter, 1987). Subsequently, psychotherapists have come to view countertransferential reactions as a potential source of clinical and diagnostic information, though still a challenge to be handled effectively within and beyond the therapy session (Pearlman & Saakvitne, 1995, p. 23).

Psychotherapeutic work carries the ongoing risk that the therapist's own issues and vulnerabilities will be stirred (Guy, 1987). We vicariously experience the pains and terrors of our clients, especially when their travails are not dissimilar to what we grapple with in our own lives. For therapists vulnerable to depression, working with depressed patients may be a challenge (Heath, 1991). In some cases, a "personal history of trauma may be reawakened by client material and may make one particularly sensitive to certain transferences or expectations from clients" (Saakvitne & Pearlman, 1996, p. 44).

A sense of inadequacy as a therapist (feeling like an "imposter") or as a person ("less than a paragon of mental health") is a particularly painful countertransferential experience for some therapists. For others, an "ego wound occurs when our treatment fails. Some of our patients, despite our best efforts, do not improve. After months or years of effort, the patient still struggles with the same conflicts and anxieties" (Freudenberger & Kurtz, 1990, p. 463).

We are charged with the challenge and responsibility to sort out the source of our countertransferential reactions. Some of our responses to a client might be similar to the reactions of others, which can be potentially useful feedback to the client. But often our reactions are simply a function of our own dynamics. It is no small task to clarify and manage these various kinds of internal responses, particularly when they are charged. Yet that is a part of our work. A cognitive–behavioral therapist, who typically is less likely to speak in terms of transference or countertransference per se, nevertheless acknowledged a desire to find

> **Why did I become angry with a patient? What does that tell me about myself, but also about them?**

language within the conceptual framework of social learning theory, to talk about the emotional experience of being a therapist. . . . Why did I become angry with a patient? What does that tell me about myself, but also about them? Why would I be sad when I've left a session? Any reason why I feel confused or anxious about somebody? How do I think about all of this within my own framework? (Zeiss, 1996)

JOURNAL ENTRY

- ✎ What has been your most significant countertransferential experience?
- ✎ What do you know and understand about your own dynamics in terms of your reactions and interactions in response to particular client dynamics?
- ✎ Have you found yourself tempted to avoid or deny certain countertransferential feelings?
- ✎ Do you feel you've grown in better understanding your countertransferential responses?
- ✎ What factors may stimulate these reactions?

BUSINESS-RELATED CONCERNS

Values and Goals

Periodic assessment of the costs and benefits of our work life is part of the process of balancing our professional and personal selves.

There is a distinction between making a living—and living; there are trade-offs. Achievement, career development, an increased standard of living, upward mobility, status, and prestige all come at a price, in terms of amount of work, pressure, and physical and psychological tolls. Our values and goals, whether conscious or not, clearly influence how we invest our energy and other resources. As Freudenberger and Robbins (1979) stated, "Can the professional put some limit on his consumer needs so that they do not spend or use him up prematurely?" (p. 290). Mahoney (1997) spoke to the conscious decision of

> giving myself permission not to earn so much money, which really made a difference. I make a comfortable living, but I have a number of friends who are in full-time practice who I would estimate make at least three times my income, and enjoy their homes and cars and travel and so on. I've been fortunate enough to be able to travel without it costing me a lot. Other things don't feel as important as the satisfaction I get from teaching and being a part-time therapist.

Career crises result when our reality and our professional values and goals come into conflict. When we experience a career crisis, we must take the time to look at the external and personal factors involved and consider options for making changes to enable us to feel better about our professional life: As Palumbo (2000) observed, "In other words, it's a chance to do in your life what we ask our clients to risk doing in theirs. Seems only fair, doesn't it?" (p. 69).

Being recognized as a busy, successful professional can be seductive. Wallerstein (1981, as cited in Millon et al., 1986, p. 125) described the potentially intensifying pace of success:

> Success and recognition breed more of the same, and with them come materialistic gains. In time the practitioner achieves what he or she has set out to achieve; a respected position in a useful profession and an enviable standard of living. Soon the boundaries of practice begin to stretch and encroach on other activities. It is the unusual clinician who can put the brakes on opportunities for successful expansion —more patients, a few additional evenings a week, a prestigious consultationship or two, just this additional course to teach, and so on. (Wallerstein, 1981). Before long the business of building a successful practice has taken over, consuming time and activities.

> I just have too much to do, and it's all good. It's like having too much good food to eat, and I'm really tired of it. . . . This is a self-care crisis as we speak. (Casey, 1997)

JOURNAL ENTRY

- How do you define "standard of living" for yourself and your family?
- How much income do you want?
- How much income do you need?
- How much can you work, and for how long?
- How many hours feel manageable, and what feels unmanageable?
- How many and what kinds of tasks can you manage?
- What signals for you the fine line between being stimulated versus being overwhelmed?
- What percentage of your time would you like to ideally dedicate to your professional life, your family life, and your self-care?
- Have you ever experienced a career crisis? If so, what did you learn?
- What was helpful in the process?
- What actions would you take should you experience such crisis either for the first time or again?
- Does the notion of controlling your success make sense to you?
- Does it fit with your experience?
- Has managing success ever felt challenging?
- How would you know if your success was becoming too costly?

Financial Matters

In developing and maintaining a practice, responsibilities range from the business of the everyday, to emergency and crisis management, to retirement planning (Goldman & Stricker, 1981). Financial duties in private practice include setting and collecting fees, maintaining financial records, budgeting, and paying estimated quarterly taxes. For many therapists, "It's a strain to do the business . . . as well as the clinical . . . and keep those separate, but also integrate them so that the relationship between them can be handled. . . . It's hard to make the shift" (Goldstone, 1996).

Most psychologists are not in the field for "big money." Likewise, many psychologists do not identify or describe themselves as businessmen or businesswomen. Nonetheless, we need to be adequately compensated for the work we do. Berger (1995) referred to a "transformation from 'neurotic helping' fueled by rescue fantasies to a work experience that [is] a fair exchange between what was given and received" (p. 317).

We need to stay aware of what is good-enough payment and what is not (Parvin & Anderson, 1999). Women therapists have reported that some clients seem to view them as needing less money, perhaps presuming that a female therapist is less serious about her profession or supported by her husband. Inadequate financial remuneration, actual or perceived, is an undeniable source of stress and potential burnout. Underlying resentment about a client's unpaid bills can affect the therapy directly or indirectly. Canter and Freudenberger (1990) noted that

> Fees and their collection provide the practitioner with the structural support needed to furnish services and fulfill professional potential. (p. 231) . . . It is critical that you come to the conclusion that you are worth what you charge, that you deserve the compensation, and that your fees seem appropriate to you. . . . In addition to the working through of money attitudes and self-worth, you should consider the level of your training and credentialing and the breadth and depth of your experience—all of which reflect on the value of your services and should be involved in any decision about fees. (p. 219)

Independent practice also involves dealing with a potentially variable income or cash flow and periods of reduced billable hours. It can be very anxiety provoking trying to determine whether variations in income and clinical hours are normal, temporary fluctuations or indicative of more serious, ongoing changes in the marketplace.

Many psychologists use the payment-at-time-of service model to minimize accruing bills for either the client or the therapist. This method has the secondary benefit of facilitating cash flow, an issue for the self-employed therapist.

We also need to determine our policy and procedures regarding a sliding fee scale. Many potential clients ask about the possibility of a sliding-scale arrangement. In some cases, clients' need may be real. In other cases, need may be more related to issues of money management, priorities, and entitlement. We need to be clear about what feels fair—to the client and to our self.

Parvin and Anderson (1999) reported that the primary ethical dilemmas of psychologists involve matters related to finances. Such dilemmas include "billing for no-shows, billing family therapy as if it were individual, distorting a patient's condition so that it qualifies for coverage, signing forms for unlicensed staff, and not collecting co-payments" (Pope & Vetter, 1992, p. 401).

JOURNAL ENTRY

- What has been your own experience in setting fees and collecting payment for your work?
- How stressful is this part of the work for you?
- What have you learned about yourself, your needs and your limits, in the process?

Practice Development

Doing clinical work is one thing. Generating a practice is another. Therapists' character sensitivity may be one of the reasons we have difficulty with the rough-and-tumble of the marketing and business demands of a psychotherapy practice (personal communication, E. S. Schlosser, August 10, 1999).

In areas where well-trained therapists are plentiful, private practitioners grapple with ongoing questions about how to be visible and "competitive enough" in the marketplace. It takes a fair amount of psychological and physical effort and energy to do what's necessary to generate referrals to maintain a business. Therapists must ask themselves, "What can I do to professionally thrive that is ego-syntonic with myself as a therapist and as a person?" Personality factors, such as extroversion and competitiveness, along with entrepreneurial acumen, do make a difference.

JOURNAL ENTRY

- ✎ What is your own experience in promoting your private practice?
- ✎ What has been helpful in promoting your practice?
- ✎ Has this changed over time?

Risk Management and Prevention

Responsibly managing risk involves taking time to periodically review matters related to the ethics of clinical practice. Neglecting such matters will at the very least, cause anxiety; at worst, we risk professional and ultimately personal liability.

Although psychologists report concern about the risk of lawsuits, the likelihood of facing a lawsuit is, in fact, statistically quite minimal. We are far more likely to be the target of a complaint filed by a disgruntled patient with our licencing board; which is for the patient to do (Bennett, cited in Shapiro, 1997).

Thus, risk management is a part of the job of being a psychotherapist. We need to be informed and proactive about documentation and record keeping, which are especially important in cases involving confidentiality, informed consent, contested divorce or custody, third-party involvement (financial or otherwise), patient trauma or abuse, and risk of harm to a client's self or anyone else (Bennett, Bryant, VandenBos, & Greenwood, 1990; Welch, 1998). In situations of concern, obtaining the necessary information and consultation will enable us to prevent problems and intervene, if and as needed (Gormanous, cited in Shapiro, 1997).

JOURNAL ENTRY

✎ What have you done to protect yourself from professional risk?
✎ Have you done as much as you think you should do?
✎ Are there other steps that might be prudent?
✎ What has precluded your taking those steps to date?
✎ What might be a source of support or assistance in this process?

Press to Develop New Markets

For therapists in private practice, there is pressure to develop new markets or to be more entrepreneurial. This appeals to some practitioners. It's one thing to decide to expand and diversify into new markets out of desire and interest, it is quite another to do so under duress as a response to infringing market forces like managed care.

The need to develop new markets may involve a major shift in thinking, action, and identity for many of us. It may entail developing new areas of clinical expertise and working with new and different clientele. It may involve restructuring our practice. It probably will involve considerable trial and error, which can be hard, especially for more established therapists who have reached a level of success and anticipated a more stable professional life by middle age. Personality factors also make a difference. More extroverted therapists may be more comfortable in dealing with a new and competitive market place and may even find the challenges stimulating.

A recent trend is the expanded application of psychology to new markets beyond the traditional "pathological" clientele. Ackley (1997), Kovacs (1997), and others have advocated the benefits "normalizing" psychological services for availability to broader markets, coaching being just one example.

JOURNAL ENTRY

✎ What has been helpful as you have redeveloped or expanded your practice?
✎ Have you lost clientele with the market changes in recent years?
✎ What has been your own experience in developing new markets?

Contemporary Pressures on Practicing Psychologists

INSTITUTIONAL EMPLOYEE STRESS

Working as a clinician in an institutional setting entails a particular set of demands, stresses, and challenges. Bureaucratic red tape and tight budgets are the norm. In many cases, "institutional rules and restrictions, excessive workloads, and organizational politics add to the despair of treating recalcitrant or otherwise unsatisfying patients" (Millon et al., 1986, p. 125). We have to make judgment calls as to which battles to fight. Freudenberger and Robbins (1979) noted that

> the survival techniques the therapist often acquires, with a kind of cynicism, in the institutional scene are many. Not the least of these are the "tricks of the trade" he learns. . . . He carefully avoids risking such labels as "acting out" or "impulse ridden" being tacked on to him. He notices that it is wise and more prudent to appear perhaps even a little dull, to appear compulsive, conformist, controlled and safe. (pp. 178–179)

In a study of therapist self-care methods, Brady, Norcross, and Guy (1995) found "making organizational changes a practice" the least commonly implemented. Guy and Norcross (1998) thereby encouraged therapists to stay conscious of institutional dynamics, and to not overlook "systemic forces inside and outside" of the office (p. 391).

Systemic factors are major forces in the well-being of employed therapists (Cherniss & Danzig, 1986; L. Miller, 1998; Saakvitne & Pearlman, 1996). Employed clinicians fare better when the work setting has an atmosphere that is respectful of clinicians and clients; a good "fit" between individual and organization values and ethics; collegial support and collaboration; supervision options; forums to address clinical issues; and mental health benefits, such as adequate space and time as necessary.

At the same time, many practitioners working in institutions and agencies confront a decreasing number of employment opportunities for PhD psychology (clinical) positions in federal and state health care (APA, 1996), tightening or dwindling agency resources, increased clinical and administrative responsibilities, decreased administrative assistance, inadequate qualified supervision, insufficient continuing education, a short of time off the beeper, and threats of job loss because of buyouts and mergers.

JOURNAL ENTRY

✎ If you are presently employed in an agency or institutional setting, how satisfied are you with your present work situation?

✎ How supportive is the setting in terms of your personal and
professional well-being?

✎ Which of your needs are being met? Which are not?

✎ What has been helpful in dealing with and addressing problematic organizational dynamics?

✎ What remains of concern?

✎ What options exist in addressing these concerns?

✎ What resources might be helpful or supportive in the process?

CHANGING HEALTH CARE MARKET

Psychologists of virtually all ages and stages have been affected by
the changing health care market of the past few decades. Change
has characterized virtually every aspect of mental health care:

> It universally is acknowledged that the mental health
> professions have changed dramatically over the last decade,
> and are continuing to change at near "warp" speed. The
> fiscal structures for and organizational settings which
> provide psychological services continue to mutate. . . . These
> changes, somewhat akin to a corporate revolution in the
> development of the profession, have prompted a
> metamorphosis for psychologists. The process of change has
> been a struggle for all, and distress inducing for many
> practitioners. The net result for many psychologists has been
> uncertainty accompanied by a sense of personal
> vulnerability. (Ginsburg, 1997, p. 4)

It universally
is acknowl-
edged that
the mental
health profes-
sions have
changed dra-
matically
over the last
decade, and
are continu-
ing to change
at near "warp"
speed.

The encroachment and interference of managed care and insurance companies have resulted in a loss of income for both participating and nonparticipating clinicians (APA, 1996). Professional
expenses, including association fees, insurance rates, continuing
education fees, and political action committee requests, have affected income. Work schedules have become longer, though not
necessarily fuller, and competition with increased numbers and
types of mental health care providers (for example, marriage and
family therapists, alcohol counselors, social workers, sex counselors) has intensified (APA, 1996).

"Participating providers" in managed care have had to deal
with a number of limits on professional autonomy regarding treatment decisions. Restrictions are placed on the number of treatment
sessions that may not necessarily correspond with the number of
sessions indicated for positive outcome, fees have repeatedly been

reduced, amount and time spent doing paperwork has significantly increased, and collection difficulties and administrative expenses have increased.

Many therapists not participating in managed care initially have had a significantly reduced pool of non-managed care clientele. Some of us have seen our solo practices restructured into partnerships or corporations, sometimes with a multidisciplinary staff. Such changes may be enriching in some ways, but at the cost of less independence and autonomy. In institutional settings, budgetary and political pressures keep psychologists in competition with other mental health professionals. Master's-level providers can be hired at lower salaries, threatening opportunities for PhD psychologists.

Given these major economic shifts and ongoing structural changes, many of us may be tempted "to make hay while the sun shines" by working longer hours and taking less time off. This can be of risk to the physical and emotional health of our self and family.

JOURNAL ENTRY

✎ What has helped you deal with the unknowns and challenges of the changing health care market?

✎ What external resources of information and support do you have access to in addressing this challenge?

✎ What might your "inner wisdom" have to offer as a guide as well?

RISK OF LAWSUITS

With the advent of large computerized data banks, compromised doctor–patient confidentiality is a major contemporary concern. Psychologists now find themselves "in difficult situations with clients over what is ethical and how much information to include in patients' files" (O'Connor, quoted in Rabasca, 1999, p. 23).

Psychologists have also become more concerned about the increasing number of malpractice threats, lawsuits, and other risks, including "frivolous" and harassment suits (Newman, 1996):

> While the chances of a psychologist facing a liability suit are, by any measure, quite slim (three quarters of one percent), complaints to the licensing board "are a new area of risk for the psychologist." That's because it's frightfully easy for a patient to file a complaint—fill out a sheet of paper and the police power of the state takes it from there. A malpractice suit, on the other hand, is a protracted affair, often lasting four to seven years. (Bennett, quoted in Shapiro, 1997, p. 19)

Simultaneously, malpractice liability premium rates have escalated. In a national study of therapists, over two-thirds

> reported fear that a client would file a formal complaint
> against them, and about 12% reported that a client had filed
> a complaint (malpractice, ethics, licensing) against them.
> Almost 3 times as many male psychologists (about 17%) as
> female psychologists (about 6%) reported that at least one
> client filed a formal complaint against them. Of course these
> studies also have methodological limitations, but their data
> supplement the actuarial methods of estimating chances of
> being sued or otherwise facing formal complaints. (Pope,
> 1999)

Dependence on third-party payments necessitates use of diagnostic nomenclature as predicated by the American Psychiatric Association (1994) in the fourth edition of the *Diagnostic and Statistical Manual of Mental Disorders*. In truth, many clients seeking psychotherapy are more aptly described as unhappy, confused, and frustrated, rather than ill per se, and are responsibly seeking to better understand and care for themselves. Many therapists find it ethically questionable to force such clientele into an insurance-required medical classification.

JOURNAL ENTRY

- ✎ Have you dealt with the threat of a malpractice suit?
- ✎ Has the possibility of a lawsuit caused you anxiety?

SOPHISTICATED CONSUMERS

It is now common for therapists to be interviewed by consumers who are "shopping around" for psychotherapy. Such consumers often ask very specific questions about treatment efficacy and prognosis. Sometimes it's clear that we are being compared to and competing directly with close colleagues and friends!

JOURNAL ENTRY

- ✎ Have you dealt with clients who are "therapist shopping"? If so, what have been your reactions?
- ✎ If you have felt uncomfortable, how have you managed those feelings?

INFORMATION EXPLOSION

Boundless clinical information is available. Relevant clinical resources, such as the latest research, sophisticated treatment modalities, and refined assessment tools, are continually emerging. New professional materials, books, articles, conferences, and continuing education, much of it is quite appealing, continually emerge. The problem is that there is more information available than there is time to make use of it (Gergen, 1992).

Although we feel pressured to keep up to date, we are bombarded with more information than we can possibly process. We risk being overwhelmed and confused by too much material taken in too quickly, we feel remorseful about being unable to take in what is available and potentially useful, and we can easily become discouraged about even trying to stay abreast of new and available materials (Freudenberger, 1986; Gold, 2000). As a result, "Many of us feel both wise and less self-confident because we are so much more acutely aware of how much we don't know" (Treadway, 1998, pp. 57–58).

JOURNAL ENTRY

- ✎ How have you dealt with the explosion of practice-relevant information?
- ✎ What works best for you in staying as well informed and up-to-date as possible?
- ✎ Do you have further needs and unresolved concerns regarding this matter?

MEDICATION AND PSYCHOTHERAPY

Psychotropic medications are now generally recognized as helpful in altering or "resetting" dysfunctional brain chemistry. At the same time, as measured by sophisticated brain-imaging technology, evidence is mounting regarding the impact of life experience, including psychotherapy, on brain physiology and function (Vaughan, 1998). Medications are an increasing part of contemporary therapy, and we need to stay up to date about the physical and psychological effects of psychotropic medication on our clients and on psychotherapy.

JOURNAL ENTRY

- ✎ What has been helpful for you in learning more about psychotropics and about the interaction between psychotherapy and medication?
- ✎ Do you have colleagues with whom you feel comfortable discussing medications and the interplay between medication and psychotherapy?
- ✎ If not, how might you go about finding the knowledge resources you need?

Connecting With Others | 6

People live in a world with others, and they need to feel connected, validated, helped, involved, and trusting in their relationships. (Jaffee & Scott, 1984, p. 130)

Connections and relationships with others, both personally and professionally, are immensely important for our well-being as therapists (Dlugos & Friedlander, 2001; Norcross, 2000). To care for our self in relationship with others, we must actively nurture our relationships with our significant other, children, family of origin, friends, and colleagues. Connecting with others beyond our immediate circle of relationships can be equally important; participation in community organizations can help us feel connected to a larger whole.

The quality of our relationships, more than the quantity, is key. In both our personal and professional lives. Our best relationships are those in which we can be as close to our true self as possible. In such relationships, we can speak out and feel heard as we express our thoughts, feelings, and concerns beyond the role of being a therapist or good listener; we can feel valued and appreciated for our true self rather than idealized or judged; and we can feel safe in lowering our defenses but still separate and differentiated from the other. Such relationships help us tend our needs in ways that our relationships with clients cannot, and should not.

> At this stage, self-care is more interactional. It can entail reaching out, asking somebody to listen to me, doing something together.

Sometimes there's a need to be more out there, sharing, talking, venting, whatever, as a form of self-care. . . . The way I was raised, you take care of yourself. That's probably shifted for me. At this stage, self-care is more interactional. It can entail reaching out, asking somebody to listen to me, doing something together. (Hornyak, 1996)

I'm really an introvert, but last winter when I was dealing with cancer, I was writing people and asking for support. Letters—I sent at most 50. This year when I put my Christmas card list on my computer, there were between 150 and 200 people! I do write letters, and I stay in frequent contact with a lot of people!" (Stone, 1997)

Various Kinds of Relationships

On a day-to-day level, an intimate relationship with a spouse or partner provides physical and emotional companionship; support, encouragement, nurturance, and understanding; assistance with domestic duties; and help with child rearing. A relationship with a significant other, for therapists and for people in general, has benefits that are both personal and professional. As stated by Guy (1987), emotional intimacy with at least one person, be it a spouse or a friend,

> must be a top priority. . . . While it is not necessary for a psychotherapist to be married to enjoy psychic balance, it seems important for the therapist to have one or more sufficiently intimate relationships in order to provide the support, empathy, and reality testing needed for resisting the depletion and isolation associated with the practice of psychotherapy. (p. 141)

It is clearly important that "our own needs for empathy are met at home [so that] we are better protected against inadvertently reaching toward our patients to satisfy our personal longing for intimacy and contact" (Lee, 1990, p. 628). For this reason, Gabbard and Lester (1996) advocated that psychotherapists

> work diligently to create a loving environment in their personal lives so that they are not forced to seek [outside] gratification of their emotional needs . . . to have a consistently loving companion to come home to after being subjected to a roller coaster of feelings throughout the day at work. (p. xiv)

As Goldberg (1991) put it, having a relationship with a significant other provides the therapist with a "safe haven . . . a place to be less than perfect—a place to be a husband or wife, a mother or father, and/or a friend, and not a special persona with omniscient and omnipotent qualities" (p. 289).

For those therapists not in an intimate romantic relationship, desired or otherwise, it is nonetheless important to have at least one close, caring personal relationship. Given the idealization and dependence of our clients, we as therapists have all the greater need for relationships based on mutuality so as to maintain a realistic and balanced view of ourselves.

JOURNAL ENTRY

✎ Do you have one or more sufficiently intimate relationships in your life? If not, is this a long-standing or more recent situation?
✎ What have you found most helpful in terms of meeting your needs, as a human being, for connection and relationship?
✎ How do you protect against acting out those needs in your work with patients?

Nurturing the Relationship

Like everyone else, therapists and their partners must nourish and tend their relationship. Working at self–other differentiation helps us respect and appreciate the other as a separate being. We need to discuss, directly and openly, the professional hazards that may affect the relationship. We need to encourage our partners to speak up or get support in speaking out if necessary: not a minor matter in a relationship with a psychologically and verbally sophisticated therapist–partner!

Clearly both quantity and quality of time are necessary for ongoing nourishment of the relationship with our significant other. Setting aside certain times as "sacred" can help ensure that process. Beer spoke to the

> need to protect my energy for my family, which for me is number one. To be able to go home, to be able to connect with them, to be able to connect with my wife . . . means recognizing the limits of my energy, to recognize the areas that are taking away my energy, so that I can protect what's most important to me, which is my family. (1997) . . . I still find time for basketball during lunch and softball in the evening, but the time I value most is the time with my family. That part of my life is the most hectic (so many activities for them), but the most rewarding. (1999)

I still find time for basketball during lunch and softball in the evening, but the time I value most is the time with my family. That part of my life is the most hectic (so many activities for them), but the most rewarding.

JOURNAL ENTRY

✎ How much do you value, and practice, nurturing your intimate relationship?
✎ What can get in the way?
✎ Does your significant other appreciate your efforts at nurturing the relationship?
✎ What desires and aspirations do you have regarding this matter?

Relationship Stresses

The therapist's relationship with a significant other is vulnerable to a range of stresses. We deal with all the universal stresses of being part of a couple, and in addition we cope with stresses more specifically related to the profession.

A relationship with a significant other needs time—time dedicated to the relationship on a regular basis—to thrive or even survive. There are many sources of competing demands for our time as therapists. Those building and maintaining a private practice often work long and irregular hours and may be tempted to work nights or Saturdays. An unsalaried position always entails some degree of unpredictability and variability in income, affecting the family's level of comfort and sense of security. Anxiety about income, concerns about patient attrition, or fear of losing out on new referrals can all contribute to a reluctance to take time off from work, thus taking away from family time. Yet, we need to be on guard against using professional pressures, however real, to justify neglecting our significant other. Although speaking about physicians, Gabbard and Menninger (1988) noted how overwork and lack of time can be an excuse for neglecting our private life:

> The demands of practice are a convenient rationalization. Physicians work long hours to deny dependency, to eradicate any trace of aggression or destructiveness that they fear others may suspect; win the unconditional love and approval of colleagues, patients, and community; to maintain complete control; and to conquer the terror of death. It is not the demands of practice, but the physicians' compulsive character that wreaks havoc in the marriage. (p. 35)

Ability to communicate with our significant other about the day's work is limited by patient–therapist confidentiality (Guy, 1987). One therapist observed that "to share much about my work . . . was to violate the essence of confidentiality. . . . I had to imagine how I would have felt if my therapist did that." In addition, after a day of listening on the job, "emotional depletion and an associated decrease in the desire to listen empathetically reduces the psychotherapist's ability to encounter his or her spouse in an intimate, genuine fashion" (Guy, 1987, p. 109).

Difficulties with self–other differentiation and objectification of the partner, as with any other couple, may manifest in a number of ways. We may wish, consciously or unconsciously, that our partner will meet our needs, for example, by serving as a selfobject to acknowledge and recognize our achievements. After giving in the external world, we might be tempted, in the privacy of our homes, to demand that our partner tend, accommodate, and care for us. At times we may displace work-related tension onto our partner. Likewise the emotional hypersensitivity of some therapists, while useful in the therapeutic process, may in fact be a drain for a spouse to live with day in and day out.

Alternatively, we may withdraw emotionally in the privacy of our home because of a desire to be left alone and to avoid interacting or experiencing any further demands. This withdrawal can leave the partner feeling alone. For the therapist, "it may seem easier to live through the experiences of patients rather than taking the risks involved in genuine encounter and intimacy with a spouse" (Guy, 1987, p. 112).

The couple's social life may be unduly affected by the therapist's work. We may choose friends and participate in organizations centered around professional connections, whether or not that is our partner's preference or interest. When we socialize with colleagues, it can be tempting to "talk shop," which may exclude—or even bore—our partner.

We also run the risk of misdirecting or misusing our professional acumen in the relationship with our significant other. Therapists have the language, should they choose to use it, to pathologize their partner and to analyze and interpret his or her feelings away as if they were symptoms to be treated. A therapist functioning as a compulsive caretaker might cast the partner as one more person in need of caretaking and then react to the partner in this way (as in projective identification). Even more problematically, the therapist may, consciously or unconsciously, manipulate the partner, capitalizing on his or her vulnerabilities out of a drive to feel superior (Guy, 1987).

JOURNAL ENTRY

- ✎ What kind of dynamics have you observed in yourself in your intimate relationship?
- ✎ Have you grown in your ability to be aware of the dynamics you bring to this relationship?
- ✎ What have you learned about the times and situations in which you are vulnerable to regression within your intimate relationship?

Couples Therapy

Couples therapy offers therapists a means of enriching and deepening intimacy with their partners. Couples' work can provide a place and process to sort out and clarify potentially complex and complicated projections and boundary confusions, which often manifest under stress in couples' dynamics.

Couples therapy can also be threatening for the therapist as patient. Irrational feelings may get stirred "that one's marriage must be perfect and free of problems, [which] make it hard to accept the flawed, mortal nature of marriage" (Guy, 1987, p. 112). Couples therapy calls the therapist–partner to task and provides a third-party "witness" to the dynamics of the relationship and the therapist–client's defensive machinations. Couples group therapy with peers can provide further illumination and perspectives on couples' dynamics. Confidentiality is an understandably paramount concern.

Pope and Tabachnick (1994) directly address the anxieties and risks of therapist confidentiality viz-a-viz therapists being in psychotherapy themselves. With breaches of confidentiality by a therapist or another group member "potentially sensitive or damaging information about the patient may become the focus of gossip and misunderstanding among the patient's colleagues, perhaps damaging personal relationships, reputation, and career" (p. 256). Those risks increase exponentially in couples group therapy.

JOURNAL ENTRY

✎   Have you been in couples therapy as a client?
✎   What was that experience like for you, as part of a couple and as a therapist in therapy?
✎   Did you experience or learn anything about yourself as part of a couple that surprised you?
✎   What would you do differently if you were to re-enter couples' therapy?

CONNECTION WITH ONE'S CHILDREN

Having children has enhanced my empathy. (Gray, 1997)

It is a joyous experience with my 20-year-old daughter—a relationship desired, but never experienced with my own mother. (S. Mikesell, personal communication, May 1999)

> Having children has enhanced my empathy.

The children of therapists bear a special burden: "It can indeed be difficult to be the child of an 'expert' in human behavior" (Guy, 1987, p. 126). One psychologist married to another psychologist acknowledged that her child, at a difficult time, implored her parents to "Think about what it's like for me having two psychologists for parents!" Another child of two psychologists, thoughtfully reflecting on his own experience, observed that it seemed that his highly able professional parents functioned at a more primitive level of self while parenting than while plying their trade . . . so that how therapists conduct therapy may bear little resemblance to how they raise their children. My parents, amidst the chaos of six young children, extramarital affairs, career demands, divorces, and the residue of their own abused childhood, often parented in an uncontained emotional state, but at work, surrounded by their degrees, favorite art, and self-selected clients, they were composed and competent. Often they raged with and neglected each other and us kids while managing flourishing practices. They wrote and presented insightful papers, at times oblivious and impervious to dangerous "cry for help" behaviors from their children. (Kirsch, 1998, p. 72)

Clearly, therapist–parents, who often are respected and esteemed by their patients, may feel less venerated in day-to-day interactions with their own offspring. Therapist–parents feeling the needs and demands of their clientele must also deal with the reality that their "children need as much or more attention, love, and intimacy than the therapist's most disturbed patients," whether or not the children can verbalize their own needs (Guy, 1987, p. 124). Therapist–parents grapple with the reality of their own limits as parents and deal with the stereotype of "the cobbler's children going barefoot." As a psychologist and as a mother, Zeiss (1996) acknowledged feelings stirred in her relationship with her daughter:

I ought to know how to help her. But this is my daughter, and I don't want to start acting like a therapist towards her. I'm not her therapist, I'm her mother. I really need to separate those points in my life and just love her and take her to the redwoods and the ocean.

JOURNAL ENTRY

- Do you have children?
- How has it been being a therapist–parent?
- If you were to role-reverse with your children, how might you describe the experience from the child's perspective?
- How has the experience changed across time for you and for them?

CONNECTION WITH FAMILY OF ORIGIN

Relationships with family of origin for the therapist, as for others, are complex and provide feelings of connection that are deep and emotional. Family-of-origin members "often have the unique ability and freedom to be honest with their perceptions . . . since they have a sense of perspective and history with the therapist which permits them to be more open about their concerns" (Guy, 1982,

p. 142). Hence the admonition to "utilize your family-of-origin relationships to help you reality test and to confront your grandiosity. These folks will in all likelihood be honest with you if invited!" (Guy & Norcross, 1998, p. 389).

JOURNAL ENTRY

- ✎ In terms of your own roots and family of origin, do you feel connected? disconnected? proud? embarrassed? mixed feelings?
- ✎ What positive legacies have you received? Are there some less positive legacies as well?

Parents

Developing more conscious, individuated, differentiated ways of relating to our parents is a goal to which most of us aspire. Time, experience, and evolving maturity help, but the process is lifelong. It involves coming to terms with unfulfilled childhood wishes and expectations, making an effort to see one's parents in a more realistic perspective, and facing the reality of limits, both in our parents, and in our selves (Kerr & Bowen, 1988).

JOURNAL ENTRY

- ✎ Are your parents still living?
- ✎ How would you describe your relationship with each individually and with them collectively?
- ✎ How have these relationships changed over time?
- ✎ Has your sense of differentiation and individuation grown with time?
- ✎ What kinds of conflicts have you experienced any resistance in that process? How have you dealt with those conflicts over time?
- ✎ In what areas might you hope for continued growth in your relationship with your parents?

Family Dynamics of Concern

However much we may desire it, the reality is that our training and experience as therapists will not necessarily heal our own family dynamics of concern. Guy (1987) spoke to a tender issue for many therapists:

> While the tendency for therapists to attempt to resolve family issues and disputes can result in growth and positive change within the family system, its destabilizing effect may create havoc as well. Some family members may experience

the therapist's attempts . . . as intrusive, assaultive, obnoxious, and inappropriate. (p. 131)

In some cases we may feel a need to confront severe pathology in an individual family member or within the family system: "Those trained to diagnose and treat mental illness often find it increasingly hard to overlook . . . when it occurs in serious forms with the family" (Guy, 1987, p. 132). What we can do is to stay aware of and speak to individual or family problems and then carefully make an appropriate referral.

JOURNAL ENTRY

- What mental health concerns have you experienced within your family?
- Have you ever felt the need to address such problems?
- How do you feel about how you have navigated these waters?
- What has worked to your satisfaction?
- What has been harder to deal with in the process?

Family Wounds and Forgiveness

In all families, members may hurt and get hurt by each other to varying degrees. When rifts and wounds are relatively minor, apologies, forgiveness, and reconnection often follow. If wounds are deep and apologies and forgiveness don't occur, unresolved conflicts may become entrenched in the family dynamics, even across generations.

Forgiving can be "hard work for even the strongest and most willing of families" (Hargrave & Anderson, 1992, p. 151), but it is clear that forgiveness can help the forgiver at least as much as the forgiven. Enright (2001) developed a four-phase model of forgiveness that includes (a) the acknowledgment and uncovering of the anger; (b) the decision and commitment to forgive; (c) taking action through understanding, compassion, and acceptance of the pain; and (d) experiencing the relief and release from emotional imprisonment.

JOURNAL ENTRY

- How serious are the rifts and wounds within your family?
- Have you been directly or indirectly affected?
- Have apologies and forgiveness been exchanged?
- If you still feel affected by old wounds inflicted by a family member, would you consider forgiveness?
- What might a next step of that process involve for you?

CONNECTION WITH FRIENDS— PSYCHOLOGISTS AND OTHERS

Friendships are priceless. They are an important source of support, sharing, and help to keep us grounded in reality. Through egalitarian relationships, we are assisted in growing more tolerant of our own shortcomings through others' acceptance of our limitations. Even for those of us who struggle with being imperfect, through friendships, as put by Maeder (1989), we "can learn to be real, solid human beings who take true pride in genuine strengths and are able to recognize and deal with genuine weaknesses" (p. 45).

Our friends may be gratified in various ways by having a friend who is also a therapist, but they may be disappointed as well. Because our work and family activities are draining and our schedules often difficult, we may not be able to dedicate as much time to our friends as we might like. Guy (1987) observed that "since it is sometimes hard to extend such caring towards one's spouse and children with regularity, it may be all the more difficult to do so towards others outside of the family" (p. 136).

It may be difficult at times to leave the therapist role behind and get the most out of friendships. Guy spoke of therapists being "excellent conversationalists and particularly talented at putting others at ease," but also as being less comfortable expressing themselves in a self-revealing way: "As a result it is very difficult for friends to feel that they really 'know' the therapist at a meaningful, personal level" (Guy, 1987, p. 137).

JOURNAL ENTRY

- How important are friends and friendships to you?
- Has this always been the case?
- Do you feel that there is mutuality in what you give and what you receive in your friendships?
- Do you have any particular friendships that you would like to see change or grow? If so, in what ways?

Friends from outside the profession of psychotherapy can offer us an alternative perspective on various aspects of life. Friends from earlier stages of life, especially those from before we became a psychologist, can also help us integrate our present and past, professional and personal selves.

JOURNAL ENTRY

- Do your relationships with nonpsychologists feel different than your friendships with psychologists? If so, how?

✎ How have you met your nonpsychologist friends?
✎ Do you find that these friendships reflect other parts of your self beyond your professional self?

CONNECTION WITH COLLEAGUES

Relationships with our colleagues are valuable (Freudenberger & Robbins, 1979; Goldberg, 1991; Grosch & Olsen, 1994). Such relationships may be with individuals and with groups of colleagues and may be formal and informal. We get different things from our relationships in different settings, whether study groups, professional meetings, and private or peer supervision. More recently, professional listservs, news groups, and chatrooms have become an additional source of connection and communication with peers. Peer support emerged as the highest priority in a study on well-functioning psychologists (Coster & Schwebel, 1997).

Finding colleagues with whom one can be genuinely open and honest can make an immense difference: "Open sharing among peers concerning the limitations of the profession, personal mistakes or shortcomings, and common problems confronted in practice can greatly reduce the stress and dissatisfaction experienced by many therapists" (Guy, 1987, p. 267). The challenge, for some, is to manage friendships with the growing numbers of colleagues over the years. The richness of a "wonderfully extended family" is too often circumscribed by the limits of time and energy (Mahoney, 1997).

Competition dynamics are often an aspect of peer relations as well. It is not unusual to experience feelings of envy regarding a peer's abilities, achievements, professional recognition, success, lifestyle, or personal attractiveness (Kassan, 1996). For many of us, these are not easy feelings to have, tolerate, or talk about. Yet they are real. Often getting to better know those whom we envy helps us understand the trade-offs they face, facilitating a shift from an idealizing to a more realistic perspective.

With time, some collegial relationships undergo a normalized blurring of professional and social lines. Some professional relationships evolve into strong friendships, with shared interests both personally and professionally. Many people speak of the satisfactions of collegial relationships that have evolved into friendships over time. We must take care, however, to avoid blurring boundaries to generate potential referral sources.

When we receive referrals from colleagues or colleague-friends whose opinion we care about, we may feel a form of "performance pressure." Such feelings should prompt us to examine the degree and appropriateness of our evaluation anxiety and desire for validation.

JOURNAL ENTRY

- ✎ Are you satisfied with your peer relationships?
- ✎ Who is in your "close-in" circle of peers?
- ✎ What do you particularly appreciate in your relationships with these people?
- ✎ What has facilitated the growth and deepening of these relationships?
- ✎ Is there anything in a particular relationship, or in your peer relationships in general, that you might need or desire more of?
- ✎ Are you conscious of feelings of competition or envy in your peer relations?
- ✎ Is this something that has varied at different stages, personally or professionally?
- ✎ How much evaluation anxiety do you experience?
- ✎ Does the concern seem appropriate or excessive?
- ✎ What is your understanding of the source and meaning of your evaluation anxiety?

Consultation and Supervision

Whatever our level of experience, conferring with colleagues or a supervisor can help us resolve particular clinical matters of concern. Peer supervision and more formalized or structured consultation or supervision are very helpful in enabling us to care for our clients and ourselves. According to Goldberg (1992),

> There are numerous clinical and personal concerns that we do not have to and should not deal with alone. This is true whether the concern is one of self-doubt, an error of omission, or even one of commission, such as a rageful or sexual indiscretion toward a client. (p. 113)

Grosch and Olsen (1994) observed that "when transference and countertransference issues are openly and honestly discussed, inappropriate involvement with clients can be prevented" (p. 128). Welch (1999) advocated peer supervision groups to help therapists monitor their emotional stability and prevent boundary violations.

Experienced clinicians have reported valuing consultation and supervision throughout their careers (Guy & Norcross, 1998), but reaching out—particularly when the issue is particularly sensitive—is not always easy to do. We may be reluctant to risk being vulnerable before a colleague or supervisor. It takes time to develop trust within collegial and supervisory relationships, and even then it can be terribly difficult and painful to risk exposing one's vulnerabilities. A seasoned therapist noted,

Calling someone when in need, I think is a problematic thing. I can see how when I'm able to do it, it's very helpful, but it's very hard to do. I don't think people do that with me very much either, as if we're too busy, or supposedly, we don't need it anymore, or it's a source of shame.

JOURNAL ENTRY

- ✎ Do you have peer and other forms of supervision available to you?
- ✎ How safe do you feel in making use of such resources?
- ✎ What would you need to develop a consultation or supervisory relationship in which you felt able to openly express concerns?

Adjunctive Collegial Relations

Professional collaboration with other professionals, such as psychopharmacologists, internists, and couples or group therapists, can be immensely helpful and supportive of patient care. By getting different perspectives on a patient's problem, we can provide the benefits of a health care team even in relatively isolated work settings. As with most teamwork, it is important that the relationship function collaboratively rather than hierarchically.

JOURNAL ENTRY

- ✎ What has been your experience with professional collaboration?
- ✎ What seems to contribute to positive experiences in terms of patient care? In terms of your own gratification?
- ✎ What is your understanding of the factors involved when collaborative efforts have been less than positive or problematic?
- ✎ How do you feel about the blurring of professional and social relationships?
- ✎ Has the time and energy you have dedicated to pursuing collegial friendships changed at different stages of life, personally and professionally? Are there any notable patterns in those collegial relationships that later on become friendships?

CONNECTION WITH GREATER SOCIETY

Human beings benefit from the recognition that we are part of a larger whole. Many of us find a sense of connection in a strong commitment to social justice, human rights, and political causes.

Civic activism is one way of connecting with a larger community. Involvement in our neighborhood and municipality is usually beneficial in both directions. We feel gratified feeling connected, and the fabric and structure of our community is strengthened by the involvement of its citizens.

Volunteering our time, energy, and abilities in a particular area of interest or concern can be immensely fulfilling. Sharing volunteer activities with our spouse can also be very satisfying. As psychologists, we also have an expertise to share:

> Activity in the interest of our community and society at large can also yield dual benefits . . . through pro bono work for the needy or after events such as natural disasters or riots, psychologists respond to civic need by applying their professional expertise. (Coster & Schwebel, 1987, p. 11)

Professional association involvement is a way of connecting with the larger community of psychologists. Local, state, and national committee work is an "enjoyable way to counter the isolation of psychotherapy practice, and it does others good as well" (O'Connor, 2000, p. 8). Professional associations serve as potentially rich resource of professional affiliation and support.

Personality and professional life-stage affect the amount of time and energy we can dedicate to working on behalf of the larger whole. Some psychologists, especially those who are trying to establish their practices, may feel that they don't have time to be involved in such activities. For many, though, developing a practice and doing volunteer work can be complementary:

> By joining with others in APA and state and region associations in purposeful action, we derive dual personal benefits: We promote our own welfare and even empower ourselves while interacting with colleagues in what often become the equivalent of a peer-support group. (Coster & Schwebel, 1987, p. 11)

For others, a high level of involvement outside of family and work may involve some tradeoffs. The risk of burnout is always present.

As was ardently expressed by Schwebel (personal communication, September 1, 2000), "as mental health specialists, we recognize that there will never be enough of us to treat all those in need of help and the best alternative is prevention. . . . Organizations like Psychologists for Social Responsibility, National Organization of Women, Women's International League for Peace and Freedom, many organizations for or about Blacks, Hispanics, Asians, etc. offer opportunities for psychologists to become involved in trying to alleviate suffering and oppression in the spirit of APA's goal of serving human need. In the process, they become members of new "communities.'"

In truth, there are many different ways to be involved and to contribute to a larger whole, be it community or profession. It is important to give some time and thought in considering one's own preferred means and degree of involvement over time. Clearly, personality and life stage are part of that consideration.

JOURNAL ENTRY

- What kinds of volunteer activity appeal to you?
- If you have been involved in volunteer activities, in what ways has it been satisfying?
- How important has professional association involvement been for you, both philosophically and concretely?
- How has your perspective on volunteer work changed with time and experience?

Balancing Self and Other Relations

Many of us who have become therapists have a capacity, whether inborn, developed, or both, to be interested in and open to others. The challenge, as persons and as professionals, is to balance our interest in and ability to relate to others with the need to maintain connection with our own separate, individual self. For most of us, it's an ongoing process to find and re-find our balance, our fulcrum, our center of gravity that enables us to reach out and share with others while remaining connected with our own self.

Those of us who tend to others in the indirect service of our own self or narcissistic needs have an even more complex balancing act to perform. We may be successful at it if this dynamic is conscious. If, however, our compulsive caregiving is a reflexive, unconscious reaction, the interpersonal relationships we form with our clients and other will be based on unacknowledged narcissistically bruised needs. We will be unable to adequately care for others if we do so based on our own needs.

JOURNAL ENTRY

- What have you learned about the process of finding and re-finding your balance between connection with others and connection with self?
- What can disrupt that balance? What supports it?
- How much sense of control do you have in terms of your impulse to help others?
- Does it feel like a choice to you? Has it always felt that way?

✎ Are there times or settings where you experience yourself responding reflexively rather than more thoughtfully and out of choice?

MAINTAINING PERSONAL BOUNDARIES

Being connected to one's self, as well as to others, involves the practice of holding good boundaries. Paying attention to the firmness of the boundaries of those with whom we relate, personally or professionally, can help us assess how much dependency they may need or demand.

> [This] capacity to feel with people . . . I've needed to have some boundaries around that or some permission to not take it all on or see it as all of me, to learn better ways to buffer or screen a bit, so that I can feel in a way that's useful, but not be so overwhelmed by it. (Hornyak, 1996)

Resetting or renegotiating personal boundaries can take effort and energy. As with most new tasks, practice helps. It is easier, of course, to be conscious of and to work at establishing solid boundaries in new relationships. Attempting to renegotiate an enmeshed relationship, however gently and carefully we might proceed—be it with family or friends—may involve time and effort to change what is known and familiar.

In our clinical work, appropriate therapist–patient differentiation is critical, not only for the patient's well-being but also for our own. Good boundaries protect us from becoming overloaded and overwhelmed in handling patients' emotional material. As Heath (1991) noted, therapists need to remember that

> the fantasies, feelings, and phantasies (unconscious) put into them by patients belong to the patients and not to themselves, though they may well be useful, and, indeed, may well stir up what is part and parcel of the therapist's own experience. The "over-load phenomenon" can best be relieved by developing a sense of what is one's own and what is not. (pp. 97–98)

A seasoned therapist observed, "I have had to be vigilant not to assume that I know what a patient's experience is, because I may be organizing their experience through my own experience."

JOURNAL ENTRY

✎ When were you first exposed to the notion of boundaries?
✎ Does a part of you, personally or professionally, ever resist maintaining good boundaries?
✎ How do you deal with this resistance?

[This] capacity to feel with people . . . I've needed to learn better ways to buffer or screen a bit, so that I can feel in a way that's useful, but not be so overwhelmed by it

✎ How do you deal with others—patients, family, acquaintances, friends—when they resist your efforts to hold your boundaries?

THE REALITY OF LIMITS

Therapists, like all human beings, have personal vulnerabilities and limitations. Consciousness of our limits in ability, time, energy, knowledge, and financial resources can be painful when we confront the deep suffering and compelling needs of others with whom we have contact. It is hard to accept the reality of our limits when others are figuratively or literally crying for help:

> Treating . . . patients is a humbling experience; as therapists, we have to accept our human limitations. I have had to come to terms with my rescue fantasies, and to accept that I cannot save all those patients, just as I could not save my siblings and parents. (S. Perlman, 1999, p. 61)

We must be alert to and honest about our limitations when a person's needs exceed our resources or when ethical considerations come into play (for example, a conflict of interest or multiple role dynamics). Sometimes, the most considerate and caring thing we can do for another is to support that person in seeking help elsewhere. That is not always easy. We may sense the person's disappointment or feelings of rejection. "The balance between being helpful and being over-involved is difficult to maintain, even when we recognize the limits of our power to help. . . . It is so hard to let go" (Canter, 1996).

> Whatever I can give is never enough. . . . I have to balance a series of circumstances—my own self, my children, my marriage . . . my individual patients. And in any given case, I could do better with more than 24 hours a day and not have it be enough. . . . So what I have to manage the most, is the fact that I can never get there. I can never read enough. . . . There's never enough to go around. . . . I have to accept those limits and that's what I work at the most . . . trying to accept . . . trying to understand that no on can ever give enough. It's just an impossible task. . . . [Meanwhile I try] to look at the things that I accomplish, as well as the things that I have yet to accomplish or cannot accomplish. (Dzaman, 1997)

Limiting commitments may seem obvious, but many of us need to practice staying conscious of the quantity and type of commitments we make to others, personally and professionally. DeNelsky (1997) reminded us to

> Learn to say "no" to extra commitments. . . . We tell our patients this all the time. . . . It is remarkably easy to get

I could do better with more than 24 hours a day. What I have to manage the most is the fact that I can never read enough. There's never enough to go around, I have to accept those limits

overloaded by adding a commitment here, an involvement there. It is important that not every minute of the day be structured with commitments. We all need some "down time" on a regular basis. (p. 4)

The process of setting limits involves learning to tolerate the risk of disappointing other people. For some of us, there may well be a connection between our feeling pressure to limitlessly give and our difficulty feeling worthy of receiving. Many of us need to practice receiving and accepting, as well as giving: "Something is seriously wrong if you are giving out more nurturance than you are receiving. Take corrective action!" (Guy & Norcross, 1998, p. 389). "Surround yourself with people with whom you can have a positive, reciprocal relationship" (S. Mikesell, personal communication, May 1999).

JOURNAL ENTRY

- How conflicted are you about having limits? About setting limits for yourself?
- What do you understand about what drives and fuels this conflict?
- How comfortable are you receiving as well as giving?

Epilogue

Most psychologists will experience [external and internal stresses] profoundly at some points in their careers. . . . If we can normalize this and talk about it and encourage explicit discussion of these issues in training and in professional development, we have a much better shot at preventing impairment and preventing ethical and boundary violations. (Reed, quoted in Rabasca, 1999, p. 23)

Education and Training in Therapist Self-Care

Education—beginning in graduate school and as an ongoing offering of continuing education—is a primary means of preventing and combating professional distress, burnout, and impairment (O'Connor, 2001). "Psychotherapeutic work is too difficult on a daily basis for the therapist to ignore his or her own psychological sustenance for even a brief time. This fact has not been clearly enough emphasized in our graduate or ongoing training" (Berger, 1995, p. 320). Kramen-Kahn and Hansen (1998) argued, "Instead of assuming clinicians will acquire self-care behaviors somewhere along the way, proactive, secondary prevention efforts should be designed for both psychotherapists-in-training and seasoned professionals" (p. 133).

THERAPIST SELF-CARE
TRAINING MODULES

Well-planned, coherent self-care training modules need to be developed for use in graduate programs and continuing education programs that are applicable across the professional lifespan. These modules should focus on the issues of both personal and professional aspects of therapist self-care (Coster & Schwebel, 1997). Examples of such modules have already been implemented in the professional training of other health care professions such as medicine (Dickstein & Elkes, 1986) and dentistry (Graham, Howard, Fine, Scherwitz, & Wycoff, 1986).

The content of self-care training modules for graduate students and interns should address the spectrum of concerns involved in therapist self-care. It should also include the matter of the stresses of training to become a therapist—a risk in itself to self-care: "For many, achieving either academic or clinical competence—the hallmarks of a burnished professional—is gained only after considerable expense and emotional sacrifice" (Millon et al., 1986, p. 122). The risk is that the rigors of "the graduate curricula and the early postdoctoral years are so demanding that they establish a workaholic habit of life instead of a balanced one" (Coster & Schwebel, 1997, p. 11). Freudenberger (1986) described how training facilities, including universities, institutes, hospitals, and agencies,

> often either overtly or covertly encourage competition. . . . Students learn techniques to help them maneuver through training. They may observe that the values of those who will graduate are determined more by colleagues, faculty, and supervising mentors than by themselves. Within this pressured graduate school environment, certain attitudes evolve. . . . As time wears on, a tinge of callousness may creep into some lives, with accompanying varied degrees of rationalization and cynicism. (p. 139)

PROMOTING SELF-CARE IN
GRADUATE STUDENTS

Therapists in training need to "to explore the balance in their lives and to establish routines of self-care" (Mahoney, 1997, p. 13). Graduate students will benefit greatly from opportunities to experience interpersonal support, recreation, and psychotherapy as an integral part of the graduate school experience.

There is considerable evidence that the number and quality of social supports significantly mediates the stress of graduate training. Likewise, faculty are viewed "as important role models, sources of reassurance and support, and important resources of information and guidance" (Guy, 1987, p. 46). At the same time, appropriate boundaries between faculty and students are obviously essential.

> Mahoney observed, "I think that there are many myths within the training and the practice of psychotherapy that we're supposed to be self-reliant to an extent that no other human beings are expected to be. And I think that's costly. Our students and beginning therapists need to be made aware again and again in their own development, that one of the most valuable skills that you can develop is the ability to reach out and to ask for comfort or help or counsel when you need it and not just be the person that others are reaching out to. . . . That's a hard one."

Participating in psychotherapy as a patient in graduate school helps therapists in training "[gain] greater knowledge and control of themselves and, as a result, [increase] their interpersonal effectiveness with patients and faculty, family, and friends" (Kaslow & Friedman, 1984, p. 52). In addition, research, as well as common sense, indicates that "play and recreation, vacation or time off, reading, creative activities, and exercise greatly improved the overall life enjoyment of students, while helping to reduce self-perceived stress and tension" (Guy, 1987, p. 47).

A fair amount of research has addressed sexual ethics training on the graduate and internship levels, likely because of rising malpractice rates related to sexual boundary violations. Although the exposure of graduate students to such training has increased, continued promotion of this important ethical concern is needed (Hamilton & Spruill, 1999; Housman & Stake, 1999; Pope & Tabachnick, 1993; Samuel & Gorton, 1998). Hamilton and Spruil (1999) asserted that

> Faculty must lead by their examples of ethical behavior. Sexual relationships between trainees and their supervisors should be prohibited, and faculty who become aware of such behavior on the part of a colleague must act decisively to put an end to it. (p. 325)

Bridges (1994), speaking from a psychodynamic perspective, recommended that

> Training, supervision, and consultations should include equipping therapists with effective strategies for conceptualizing, containing, and managing such feelings when they arise. . . . With support and education, therapists can view eroticized transference–countertransference as any other strong affect experience in psychotherapy. When understood, sexual feelings in the treatment relationship

provide opportunities to creatively enrich and advance psychotherapy. (pp. 432–433)

Professional Association Support of Therapist Self-Care

HISTORY

In 1980 the American Psychological Association (APA) Council of Representatives passed a motion to establish a task force to address the issues of psychologist distress and impairment. The APA Advisory Committee on Impaired Psychologists was established in 1986. The committee developed a series of convention programs and produced two issues of *Assisting Impaired Psychologists* edited by Schwebel, Skorina, and Schoener (1988, rev. ed. 1994). Also in 1986, APA published *Professionals in Distress: Issues, Syndromes, and Solutions in Psychology*, edited by Kilburg, Nathan, and Thoreson. In 1996, the APA Advisory Committee on Impaired Psychologists was renamed the APA Advisory Committee on Colleague Assistance (ACCA), and its mission was broadened to address not only professional impairment but also professional stress and distress.

The 1997 APA convention included an APA Miniconvention on "Taking Care of Ourselves." This miniconvention included presentations; symposia on the issues of psychologist distress, self-care, impairment, and prevention; and achievement awards to honored psychologists for "Helping Psychologists Take Care of Themselves" (Pantano, 1997).

The APA Board of Professional Affairs has supported the broadening of ACCA's mission. It has recognized as a major need the development of proactive models of therapist self-care for dealing with the stresses of contemporary professional psychology in the service of prevention of psychologist burnout and impairment.

In the late 1990s, ACCA broadened its mission to include self-care as an issue of concern to psychologists: "Historically, colleague assistance programs in psychology focused on impaired psychologists, particularly those with mental health and substance abuse problems or medical illnesses" (Ginsburg, 1997, p. 6), but all psychologists experience some degree of distress, and self-care can help them prevent further disability or impairment. Another recent goal of ACCA has been to establish a liaison with the APA association of graduate students (APAGS; Schoener, 1999) to support and develop self-care in those entering the field.

Some of the APA divisions have shown significant leadership as well. Division 42 (Independent Practice) has offered several therapist self-care convention programs in recent years, most recently the Herbert Freudenberger Memorial Symposium (2000). The Division 42 Practice Niche Guides include a guide on "Burnout Prevention and Treatment: Helping the Helper" by Thomas M. Skovholt and Len Jennings (APA, 1999). The division has also sponsored a series of "Women's Renewal Day" programs at the culmination of midwinter conferences.

A number of APA state associations have been instrumental in offering convention and continuing education programming related to the topic (DCDA, 2002). The New York State Psychological Association recently offered a program on stress management for graduate students at its annual meeting (NOFP, 2001). Colleague assistance programs have been established by some state associations.

The Maryland Colleague Assistance Committee states as its goals:

> 1) understanding the context and experience of the psychologist requesting assistance; 2) considering the domain (i.e., distress vs. impairment, severity and intensity of the experience; 3) formulating a plan, in collaboration with the colleague psychologist, to address the issues identified; and 4) assisting and supporting them in the seeking of necessary and appropriate services, i.e., developing the appropriate and requisite knowledge, skills, and abilities to cope with and adapt to the change in the health and mental health delivery systems. (Ginsburg, 1997, p. 6)

NEED FOR FURTHER ASSOCIATION SUPPORT

Top-level APA political, financial, and administrative support is imperative and essential in the education and training of therapist self-care and the prevention of impairment. Orr (1997) noted,

> It has been estimated that state program development has reached critical mass and can no longer expand without guidance from APA . . . [including] a centralized approach that is not limited to one part of the Practice Directorate but addresses all psychologists, researchers, academicians, and clinicians alike. . . . APA standing committees would create the necessary framework to develop principles, procedures and guidelines. (p. 294)

Potential additional services at the national or state level might include the following:

- recognition of therapists who exemplify the balancing of professional and personal life (an example is the APA 2000 Presidential Citation to Dr. Karen Zager),
- listings of psychologists experienced in providing supervision to peers and to other psychologists, and
- toll-free 24-hour information and referral phone lines and one-hour free legal services.
- Ongoing columns on the topic of therapist self-care could be incorporated into professional association publications, including journals, newsletters, newsgrams, and special editions. For example, an *APA Monitor* story entitled "In Search of Balance" (APA Monitor, August 1997) included a photograph and description of a psychologist balancing his professional life with his part-time child rearing and his interest in viticulture (growing grapes to make wine).
- Various APA venues have developed listservs, news groups, interactive mailing lists, chatrooms, and Web sites that would be appropriate and valuable means of sharing material and facilitating related to therapist self-care; see http://www.apa.org for more information. More of these would extend this valuable communication to more psychologists.

References

Ablow, K. R. (1992). *To wrestle with demons: A psychiatrist struggles to understand his patients and himself.* Washington, DC: American Psychiatric Press.

Ackerley, G. D., Burnell, J., Holder, D. C., & Kurdek, L. A. (1988). Burnout among licensed psychologists. *Professional Psychology: Research and Practice, 19,* 624–631.

Ackley, D. A. (1997). *Breaking free of managed care.* New York: Guilford Press.

Adams, K. (1990). *Journal to the self: Twenty-two paths to personal growth.* New York: Warner Books.

Adams, K. (1993). *The way of the journal.* Lutherville, MD: Sidran Press.

Adams, K. (2000). *The write way to wellness: A workbook for healing and change.* Lakewood, CO: Center for Journal Therapy.

American Psychiatric Association. (1994). *Diagnostic and statistical manual of mental disorders* (4th ed.). Washington, DC: Author.

American Psychological Association. (1992). Ethical principles of psychologists and code of conduct. *American Psychologist, 47,* 1597–1611.

American Psychological Association. (1996). *Committee for the Advancement of Professional Practice (CAPP) Survey of Psychological Practitioners.* Washington, DC: Author.

Andres, M., Ebaugh, E., Feeney, J., Long, P., & Zipin, M. (2001). *Listening to the wisdom of the body.* Retreat workshop (Brochure), Xixim, Mexico.

Bacal, H. A., & Thomson, P. G. (1998). Optimal responsiveness and the therapist's reaction to the patient's unresponsiveness. In H. A. Bacal (Ed.), *Optimal responsiveness: How therapists heal their patients* (pp. 249–270). Northvale, NJ: Jason Aronson.

Baji-Holms, K. (1999). *One hundred and one vacations to change your life: A guide to wellness centers, spiritual retreats, and spas.* Secaucus, NJ: Carol.

Baker, E. K. (1984, August). *Respecting and nourishing ourselves as therapists: A psychodramatic exploration.* Workshop presented at the annual convention of the American Psychological Association, Toronto.

Baker, E. K. (1988, August). *The self of the psychotherapist: An experiential workshop.* Workshop presented at the 96th annual convention of the American Psychological Association, Atlanta.

Baker, E. K. (1989, August). *Autobiographical journaling in facilitating development of the self.* Experiential workshop presented at the 97th annual convention of the American Psychological Association, New Orleans.

Baker, E. K. (1990). Autobiographical journal writing: A resource for ourselves as therapists. *The Independent Practitioner, 10,* 30–34.

Baker, E. K., & Callahan, M. L. (2000). *Therapist self-care: Addressing our ambivalence: An experiential workshop.* Unpublished manuscript.

Baker, E. K., & Hays, K. (1986, August). *The creative and therapeutic benefits of journal writing.* Presentation at the 94th annual convention of the American Psychological Association, Washington, DC.

Baker, E. K., & O'Neil, P. (1989, January). *Journal writing: Becoming an artist at life.* Workshop presented at the National Museum of Women in the Arts, Washington, DC.

Baldwin, C. (1991). *One to one: Self-understanding through journal writing.* New York: M. Evans & Co. (Original work published 1977)

Baldwin, C. (1990). *Life's companion: Journal writing as a spiritual quest.* New York: Bantam Books.

Barnett, J. E. (1996). Boundary issues and dual relationships: Where to draw the line? *The Independent Practitioner, 16*(3), 138–140.

Barnett, J. E., & Sarnel, D. (2000, June). No time for self-care? *42 Online* [The online journal of Psychologists in Independent Practice, a division of the American Psychological Association]. Retrieved April 2, 2002 from http://www.division42.org/MembersArea/Nws_Views/articles/Ethics/no_time.html

Barron, J. W. (Ed.). (1993). *Self-analysis: Critical inquiries, personal visions.* Hillsdale, NJ: Analytic Press.

Basecu, C. (1996). The ongoing, mostly happy "crisis" of parenthood and its effect on the therapist's clinical work. In B. Gerson (Ed.), *The therapist as a person: Life crises, life choices, life experiences. and their effects on treatment* (pp. 101–117). Hillsdale, NJ: Analytic Press.

Baum, A., & Posluszny, D. M. (1999). Health psychology: Mapping biobehavioral contributions to health and illness. *Annual Review of Psychology, 50,* 137–163.

Bennett, B. E., Bryant, B. K., VandenBos, G. R., & Greenwood, A. (1990). *Professional liability and risk management.* Washington, DC: American Psychological Association.

Benson, H. (with Klipper, M. Z.). (1975). *The relaxation response.* New York: Avon.

Benson, H. (1996). *Timeless healing: The power and biology of belief.* New York: Charles Scribner's Sons.

Berger, M. (1995). Sustaining the professional self: Conversations with senior psychotherapists. In M. B. Sussman (Ed.), *A perilous calling: The hazards of psychotherapy practice* (pp. 302–321). New York: Wiley.

Bergman, S. J. (1995). Men's psychological development: A relational perspective. In R. F. Levant, & W. S. Pollack (Eds.), *A new psychology of men.* New York: Basic Books.

Berkowitz, M. (1987). Therapist survival: Maximizing generativity and minimizing burnout. *Psychotherapy in Private Practice, 5*(1), 85–89.

Blau, T. (1984). Foreword. In F. W. Kaslow (Ed.), *Psychotherapy with psychotherapists* (pp. ix–x). New York: Haworth Press.

Blechner, M. J. (1996). Psychoanalysis in and out of the closet. In B. Gerson (Ed.), *The therapist as a person: Life crises, life choices, life experiences, and their effects on treatment* (pp. 223–239). Hillsdale, NJ: Analytic Press.

Bloch, D. A. (1986). Foreword. In C. D. Scott & J. Hawk (Eds.), *Heal thyself: The health of health care professionals* (pp. vii–x). New York: Brunner/Mazel.

Blum, J. E., & Weiner, M. B. (2000, Winter). Aging today. *Independent Practitioner,* pp. 25–27.

Brady, J. L., Norcross, J. D., & Guy, J. D. (1995). Managing your own distress: Lessons from psychotherapists healing themselves. In L. VandeCreek, S. Knapp, & T. L. Jackson (Eds.), *Innovations in clinical practice* (pp. 293–306). Sarasota, FL: Professional Resource Press.

Breathnach, S. B. (2000). *The simple abundance companion.* New York: Warner Books.

Brehony, K. A. (1997). *Awakening at midlife: A guide to reviving your spirits, recreating your life, and returning to your truest self.* New York: Riverhead Books.

Brenner, M., Donovan, M. W., Dubner, M. A., & Lovett, H. (1999, April). *Creative expression in women: Poetry, drama, fiction & psychotherapy.* First annual conference between the arts and Psychotherapy. Washington, DC.

Bridges, N. A. (1994). Meaning and management of attraction: Neglected areas of psychotherapy training and practice. *Psychotherapy, 31,* 424–433.

Broughton, J. J., & Olgivie, R. D. (Eds.). (1992). *Sleep, arousal, and performance.* Boston: Birkhauser.

Burka, J. B. (1996). The therapist's body in reality and fantasy: A perspective from an overweight therapist. In B. Gerson (Ed.), *The therapist as a person: Life crises, life choices, life experiences and their effects on treatment* (pp. 255–275). Hillsdale, NJ: Analytic Press.

Cameron, J. (1998). *The right to write: An invitation and initiation into the writing life.* New York: Jeremy P. Tarcher/Putnam.

Canter, M. B. (1996, August). *Physician heal thyself? Yes, but . . .* Paper presented at the 104th annual convention of the American Psychological Association, Toronto.

Canter, M. B., & Freudenberger, H. R. (1990). Fee scheduling and monitoring. In E. Margenau (Ed.), *The encyclopedic handbook of private practice* (pp. 217–232). New York: Gardner Press.

Cantor, D. W. (1998). Achieving a mental health bill of rights. *Professional Psychology: Research and Practice, 29,* 315–316.

Cantor, D. W. (with Thompson, A.). (2001). *What do you want to do when you grow up: Starting the next chapter of your life.* New York: Little, Brown.

Cantor, D. W. & Bernay, T. (with Stoess, J.). (1992). *Women in power.* Boston: Houghton-Mifflin.

Caplan, G., & Caplan, R. (2001). *Helping the helpers not to harm: Iatrogenic damage and community mental health.* Philadelphia: Brunner/Routledge.

Celenza, A. (1998). Precursors to therapist sexual misconduct: Preliminary findings. *Psychoanalytic Psychology, 15,* 378–395.

Chasin, B. (1996). Death of a psychoanalyst's child. In B. Gerson (Ed.), *The therapist as a person: Life crises, life choices, life experiences, and their effects on treatment* (pp. 3–20). Hillsdale, NJ: Analytic Press

Chernin, K. (1994). *In my mother's house.* New York: HarperPerennial.

Cherniss, C. (1995). *Beyond burnout.* New York: Routledge.

Cherniss, C., & Danzig, S. A. (1986). Preventing and managing job-related stress. In R. R. Kilburg, P. E. Nathan, & R. W. Thoreson (Eds.), *Professionals in distress: Issues, syndromes and solutions in psychology* (pp. 255–273). Washington, DC: American Psychological Association.

Comas-Diaz, L., & Griffin, E. E. H. (Eds.). (1988). *Clinical guidelines in crosscultural mental health.* New York: Wiley.

Cooper, D. A. (1999). *Silence, simplicity and solitude: A complete guide to spiritual retreat.* Woodstock, VT: SkyLight Paths.

Coster, J. C., & Schwebel, M. (1997). Wellfunctioning in professional psychologists. *Professional Psychology: Research and Practice, 28,* 5–14.

Courtois, C. A. (1999). *Recollection of sexual abuse: Treatment principles and guidelines.* New York: W. W. Norton.

Covatta, A. (1998). Opening a new year. *Centerpoint, 6,* 1.

Cramer, P. (2000). Defense mechanisms in psychology today. *American Psychologist, 55,* 637–645.

Dement, W. C. (1999). *The promise of sleep.* New York: Dell.

DeNelsky, G. V. (1997, August). *Taking care of your physical health: Smoking and stress reduction.* Paper presented at the 105th annual convention of the American Psychological Association, Chicago.

Dickstein, L. F., & Elkes, J. (1986). A health awareness workshop: Enhancing coping skills in medical students. In C. D. Scott & J. Hawk (Eds.), *Heal thyself: The health of health care professionals* (pp. 269–281). New York: Brunner/Mazel.

Dlugos, R. F., & Friedlander, M. L. (2001). Passionately committed psychotherapists—A qualitative study of their experiences. *Professional Psychology: Research and Practice, 32,* 298–308.

Domar, A. D. (with Dreher, H.). (2000). *Self-nurture: Learning to care for yourself as effectively as you care for everyone else.* New York: Viking.

Donovan, M. (1996, August). *Demeter and Persephone revisited: Ambivalence and separation in the mother–daughter relationship.* Paper presented at the 104th annual convention of the American Psychological Association, Toronto.

Edelwich, J. (with Brodsky, A.). (1980). *Burnout: Stages of disillusionment in the helping professions.* New York: Human Science Press.

Edelwich, J. (with Brodsky, A.). (1982). *Sexual dilemmas for the helping professional.* New York: Brunner/Mazel.

Elliott, D. M., & Guy, J. D. (1993). Mental health professions versus non-mental health professionals: Childhood trauma and adult functioning. *Professional Psychology: Research and Practice, 24,* 83–90.

Emmett, S. W. (1999). Spirituality, self-care and the therapist. *The Perspective: A Professional Journal of the Renfrew Center Foundation, 5,* 10–13.

Enright, R. D. (2001). *Forgiveness is a choice.* Washington, DC: American Psychological Association.

Erikson, E. H. (1963). *Childhood and society.* New York: W. W. Norton. (Original work published 1952)

Farber, B. A. (1963). The satisfactions and stresses of psychotherapeutic work: A factor analytic study. *Professional Psychology, 12,* 621–628.

Federal Interagency Forum on Aging-Related Statistics. (2000, August 10). Well-being improves for most older people, but not for all, new federal report says. [Press release] pp. 1–4.

Field, J. (1981). *A life of one's own.* Los Angeles: Jeremy P. Tarcher.

Figley, C. R. (Ed.). (1995). *Compassion fatigue: Coping with secondary traumatic stress disorder in those who treat the traumatized.* New York: Brunner/Mazel.

Flannery, R. B. (1987). From victim to survivor: A stress management approach in the treatment of learned helplessness. In B. A. van der Kolk (Ed.), *Psychological trauma* (pp. 217–232). Washington, DC: American Psychiatric Press.

Fowler, R. D. (2000). A lesson in taking our own advice. *Monitor on Psychology, 31*(2), 9.

Frank, K. A. (1977). *The human dimension in psychoanalytic practice.* New York: Grune & Stratton.

Frankl, V. (1969). *Man's search for meaning: An introduction to logotherapy.* New York: Washington Square Press.

Fraser, J. A. (2001, February 4). They don't call it a cell for nothing—Phone, fax and laptop keep us tied to our jobs. *Washington Post,* p. B2.

Freudenberger, H. J. (1974). Staff burnout. *Journal of Social Issues, 30,* 159–165.

Freudenberger, H. J. (1975). The staff burnout syndrome in alternative institutions. *Psychotherapy: Theory, Research and Practice, 12,* 72–83.

Freudenberger, H. J. (1984). Impaired clinicians: Coping with burnout. In P. A. Keller & L. Ritt (Eds.), *Innovations in clinical practice: A source book* (Vol. 3, pp. 223–227). Sarasota, FL: Professional Resource Exchange.

Freudenberger, H. J. (1985). The health professional in treatment: Symptoms, dynamics, and treatment issues. In C. D. Scott & J. Howth (Eds.), *Heal thyself: The health of healthcare professionals* (pp. 185–193). New York: Brunner Mazel.

Freudenberger, H. J. (1986). Chemical abuse among psychologists: Symptoms, causes and treatment issues. In R. R. Kilburg, P. E. Nathan, & R. W. Thoreson (Eds.), *Professionals in distress: Issues, syndromes, and solutions in psychology* (pp. 135–152). Washington, DC: American Psychological Association.

Freudenberger, H. J., & Kurtz, T. (1990). Risks and rewards of independent practice. In E. A. Margenau (Ed.), *The encyclopedic handbook of private practice* (pp. 461–472). New York: Gardner Press.

Freudenberger, H. J., & Robbins, A. (1979). *The hazards of being a psychoanalyst. Psychoanalytic Review, 66,* 275–296.

Gabbard, G. O., & Lester, E. P. (1996). *Boundaries and boundary violations in psychoanalysis.* New York: Basic Books.

Gabbard, G. O., & Menninger, R. W. (Eds.). (1988). *Medical marriages.* Washington, DC: American Psychiatric Press.

Gergen, K. J. (1992). *The saturated self: Dilemmas of identity in contemporary life.* New York: Basic Books.

Gerson, B. (Ed.). (1996). *The therapist as a person: Life crises, life choices, life experiences, and their effects on treatment.* Hillsdale, NJ: Analytic Press.

Ginsburg, M. R. (1997, August). Colleague assistance programs in psychology: How we can help. Paper presented at the 105th annual convention of the

American Psychological Association, Chicago.

Gold, H. (2000). *Division leadership—Midwinter meeting*. Division 42 Listserv, Retrieved November 22, 2000, from http://www.division42.org

Goldberg, C. (1991). *On being a psychotherapist*. Northvale, NJ: Jason Aronson.

Goldberg, C. (1992). *The seasoned psychotherapist: Triumph over adversity*. New York: W. W. Norton.

Goldfried, M. (Ed.). (2001). *How therapists change: Personal and professional reflections*. Washington, DC: American Psychological Association.

Goldman, G. D., & Stricker, G. (Eds.). (1981). *Practical problems of a private psychotherapy practice*. New York: Jason Aronson.

Graham, L. E., Howard, C. E., Fine, J. I., Scherwitz, L., & Wycoff, S. F. (1986). Developing a school of dentistry wellness program at the University of California, San Francisco. In C. D. Scott & J. Hawk (Eds.), *Heal thyself: The health of health care professionals* (pp. 282–295). New York: Brunner/Mazel.

Greenspan, B. (1999, Spring). A garden of opportunities: Personal writing for therapists. *The Perspective: A Professional Journal of the Renfrew Center Foundation, 5*(1), 4–6.

Grosch, W. N., & Olsen, D. C. (1994). *When helping starts to hurt*. New York: W. W. Norton.

Grosch, W. N., & Olsen, D. C. (1995). Prevention: Avoiding burnout. In M. B. Sussman (Ed.), *A perilous calling: The hazards of psychotherapy practice* (pp. 275–287). New York: Wiley.

Guy, J. D. (1987). *The personal life of the psychotherapist*. New York: Wiley.

Guy, J. D. (1996, August). Spiritual and religious methods. In J. C. Norcross (Chair), *Leaving it at the office: How psychologists replenish themselves*. Symposium conducted at the 104th annual convention of the American Psychological Association, Toronto.

Guy, J. D. (2000). Holding the holding environment together: Self-psychology and psychotherapist care. *Professional Psychology: Research and Practice, 31*, 351–352.

Guy, J. D., & Norcross, J. C. (1998). Therapist self-care checklist. In G. P.

Koocher, J. C. Norcross, & S. S. Hill, III (Eds.), *Psychologists' desk reference* (pp. 281–392). New York: Oxford University Press.

Guy, J. D., Poelstra, P. L., & Stark, M. J. (1989). Personal distress among psychotherapists: A national survey of its incidence, etiology, impact, and treatment. *Professional Psychology: Research and Practice, 20*, 40–50.

Hadler, S. J. (1997). Seeds. *Voices: The Art and Science of Psychotherapy, 33*(4), 31–38.

Hagan, K. L. (1990). *Internal affairs: A journalkeeping workbook for self-intimacy*. San Francisco: Harper & Row.

Hahn, H. (1987). *The International Women's Writing Guild presents first biennial artist of life award* (News release). New York: International Women's Writing Guild.

Hamilton, J. C., & Spruill, J. (1999). Identifying and reducing risk factors related to trainee-client sexual misconduct. *Professional Psychology: Research & Practice, 30*, 318–327.

Hargrave, T. D., & Anderson, W. T. (1992). *Finishing well: Aging and reparation in the intergenerational family*. New York: Brunner/Mazel.

Hays, K. (1997, August). *Keeping the equipment humming: Taking care of your physical health*. Paper presented at the 105th annual convention of the American Psychological Association, Chicago.

Heath, S. (1991). *Dealing with the therapist's vulnerability to depression*. Northvale, NJ: Jason Aronson.

Helms, J. E., & Cook, D. A. (1999). *Using race and culture in counseling and psychotherapy: Theory and process*. Boston: Allyn and Bacon.

Hilton, R. (1997). The healing process for therapists: Some principles of healing and self recovery. In L. E. Hedges, R. Hilton, V. S. Hilton, & O. B. Caudill, Jr. (Eds.), *Therapists at risk: Perils of the intimacy of the therapeutic relationship* (pp. 147–157). Northvale, NJ: Jason Aronson.

Holmes, T. H., & Rahe, R. H. (1967). The social readjustment rating scale. *Journal of Psychosomatic Research, 11*, 213–218.

Hornyak, L. M., & Baker, E. K. (1989). *Experiential therapies for eating disorders*. New York: Guilford Press.

Housman, L. M., & Stake, J. E. (1999). The current state of sexual ethics training in clinical psychology: Issues of quantity, quality, and effectiveness. *Professional Psychology: Research and Practice, 30*, 302–311.

Hudson, F. M. (1991). *The adult years.* San Francisco: Jossey-Bass.

In search of balance. (1997, August). *APA Monitor*, p. 60.

Jaffee, D. T., & Scott, C. D. (1984). *From burnout to balance: A workbook for peak performance and self-renewal.* New York: McGraw-Hill.

Jamison, K. R. (1996). *An unquiet mind.* New York: Random House.

Jeffords, J. M. (1999). Confidentiality of medical information: Protecting privacy in an electronic age. *Professional Psychology: Research and Practice, 30*(2), 31–35.

Jones, S. E. (1992). The working psychologist in personal crisis. *Psychotherapy in Private Practice, 11*(3), 31–35.

Jordan, J. V., Kaplan, A. G., & Surrey, J. L. (1990). *Empathy revisited.* Wellesley, MA: Stone Center.

Jordan, J. V., Miller, J., Stiver, I., Surrey, J. L., & Kaplan, A. G. (1991). *Women's growth in connection.* New York: Guilford Press.

Jurkovic, G. J. (1997). *Lost childhoods: The plight of the parentified child.* New York: Brunner/Mazel.

Kabat-Zinn, J. (1994). *Wherever you go, there you are: Mindfulness meditation in everyday life.* New York: Hyperion.

Kahn, S., & Fromm, E. (Eds.). (2001). *Changes in the therapist.* Mahwah, NJ: Erlbaum.

Kaslow, F. W. (Ed.). (1984). *Psychotherapy with psychotherapists.* New York: Haworth Press.

Kaslow, N. J., & Friedman, D. (1984). The interface of personal treatment and clinical training for psychotherapy trainees. In F. W. Kaslow (Ed.), *Psychotherapy with psychotherapists* (pp. 33–57). New York: Haworth Press.

Kassan, L. D. (1996). *Shrink rap: Sixty psychotherapists discuss their work, their lives, and the state of their field.* Northvale, NJ: Jason Aronson.

Kearney-Cooke, A., & Hill, L. (1994, November). Renewing the inner spirit: Finding balance in our personal and professional lives. Workshop, Philadelphia.

Kearney-Cooke, A., & Rabinor, J. (1994, November). *Rituals for renewal: Caring for caregivers.* Keynote presentation at the Fourth Renfrew Foundation Conference, Philadelphia.

Kerr, M. E., & Bowen, M. (1988). *Family evaluation: An approach based on Bowen theory.* New York: W. W. Norton.

Kesten, D. (2001). *The healing secrets of food: A practical guide for nourishing body, mind, and soul.* Novato, CA: New World Library.

Kiecolt-Glaser, J. K. (1999). Stress, personal relationships, and immune function: Health implications. *Brain, Behavior, and Immunity, 13*(1), 61–72.

Kohlberg, L. A. (1967). Moral and religious education and the public schools: A developmental view. In T. Sizer (Ed.), *Religion and public education.* Boston: Houghton-Mifflin.

Kohut, H. (1971). *The analysis of the self.* New York: International Universities Press.

Kohut, H. (1984). *How does analysis cure?* New York: International Universities Press.

Kottler, J. A. (1993). *On being a therapist* (rev. ed.). San Francisco, CA: Jossey-Bass.

Kottler, J. A., & Hazler, R. J. (1997). *What you never learned in graduate school: A survival guide for therapists.* New York: W. W. Norton.

Kovacs, A. L. (1997, August). *Pursuing the impossible: Reflections on the hazards of practicing psychotherapy.* Paper presented at the 105th annual convention of the American Psychological Association, Chicago.

Kramen-Kahn, B., & Hansen, N. D. (1998). Rafting the rapids: Occupational hazards, rewards, and coping strategies of psychotherapists. *Professional Psychology: Research and Practice, 29*, 130–134.

Labier, D. (2000). *Modern madness: The hidden link between work and emotional conflict.* Lincoln, NE: iUniverse.com.

Lachman, M. E., & James, J. B. (Eds.). (1997). *Multiple paths of midlife development.* Chicago: University of Chicago Press.

Lassiter, J. F. (1990). A minority experience of private practice. In E. Margenau (Ed.), *The encyclopedic handbook of private practice* (pp. 596–607). New York: Gardner Press.

Lederman, E. (1998). *Vacations that can change your life: Adventures, retreats and workshops for mind, body and spirit.* Naperville, IL: Sourcebooks.

Lee, A. C. (1990). Women therapists: Special issues in professional and personal lives. In E. Margenau (Ed.), *The encyclopedic handbook of private practice* (pp. 619–632). New York: Gardner Press.

Levant, R. F., & Pollock, W. S. ((Eds). (1995). *A new psychology of men.* New York: Basic Books.

Levinson, D. J. (1978). *The seasons of a man's life.* New York: Ballantine Books.

Lindner, H. (1990). How to deal with emotional issues upon retirement or termination of practice. In E. Margenau (Ed.), *The encyclopedic handbook of private practice* (pp. 560–567). New York: Gardner Press.

Lundien E., & Geiger, L. A. (1999). Thoughts on succeeding in practice. *The Independent Practitioner, Winter 1999,* 18–20.

Maeder, T. (1989, January). Wounded healers. *Atlantic Monthly,* pp. 37–47.

Mahler, M. (1968). *On human symbiosis and vicissitudes of individuation.* New York: International Universities Press.

Mahoney, M. J. (1995, July). *The personal life of the psychotherapist.* Paper presented at the meeting of the IV European Congress of Psychology, Athens, Greece.

Mahoney, M. J. (1997). Psychotherapists' personal problems and self-care patterns. *Professional Psychology: Research and Practice, 28,* 14–16.

Mahoney, M. J. (1998). Essential themes in the training of psychotherapists. *Psychotherapy in Private Practice, 17*(1), 43–59.

Manning, M. A. (1994). *Undercurrents: A life beneath the surface.* San Francisco, CA: HarperSanFrancisco.

Maslach, C. (1986). Stress, burnout, and alcoholism. In R. R. Kilburg, P. E. Nathan, & R. W. Thoreson (Eds.), *Professionals in distress: Issues, syndromes, and solutions in psychology* (pp. 53–75). Washington, DC: American Psychological Association.

Maslach, C., & Leiter, M. P. (1999, September/October). Take this job and . . . love it! *Psychology,* pp. 50–53, 78–80.

Maslow, A. H. (1968). *Toward a psychology of being* (2nd ed.). New York: Van Nostrand Reinhold.

McKay, M., Beck, K., & Sutker, C. (2001). *The self-nourishment companion: 52 inspiring ways to take care of yourself.* Oakland, CA: New Harbinger.

Miller, A. (1981). *The drama of the gifted child.* New York: Basic Books.

Miller, J. (1987). *Toward a new psychology of women.* Boston: Beacon Press.

Miller, J. B., Jordan, J. V., Kaplan, A., Stiver, I. P., & Surrey, J. L. (1991). *Some misconceptions and reconceptions of a relational approach.* Wellesley, MA: Stone Center.

Miller, L. (1998). Our own medicine: Traumatized psychotherapists and the stress of doing therapy. *Psychotherapy, 35*(2), 137–146.

Miller, W. R. (Ed.). (1999). *Integrating spirituality into treatment: Resources for practitioners.* Washington, DC: American Psychological Association.

Millon, T., Millon, C., & Antoni, M. (1986). Professionals in distress. In R. R. Kilburg, P. E. Nathan, & R. W. Thoreson (Eds.), *Professionals in distress: Issues, syndromes, and solutions in psychology* (pp. 119–134). Washington, DC: American Psychological Association.

Montgomery, L. M., Cupit, B. E., & Wimberley, T. K. (1999). Complaints, malpractice, and risk management: Professional issues and personal experiences. *Professional Psychology: Research and Practice, 30*(4), 402–410.

Moore, T. (1994). *Care of the soul: A guide for cultivating depth and sacredness in everyday life.* New York: Harper Perennial.

Moore, T. (2001, August). *Spirituality and psychology: Care of self, spirit, and soul.* Workshop presented at the Eighteenth Annual Cape Cod Summer Symposium, Eastham, MA.

Murray, B. (1998, March). Data smog: Newest culprit in brain drain. *APA Monitor,* pp. 1, 48.

Nagayama-Hall, G. C., & Maramba, G. G. (2001). In search of cultural diversity: Recent literature in cross-cultural and ethnic minority psychology. *Cultural Diversity and Ethnic Minority Psychology, 7*(1), 12–26.

Newman, M. (1996). Practitioner survey yields useful results. *Monitor on Psychology, 27*(6), 27.

New York State Psychological Association Organization of Future Psychologists [NOFP]. (2001, May). Caring for our own: Stress-Management for graduate students. Workshop presented at the 3rd annual student miniconvention of the New York State Psychological Association, Albany, NY.

Norcross, J. C. (2000). Psychotherapist self-care: Practitioner-tested, research-informed strategies. *Professional Psychology: Research and Practice, 31,* 710–713.

Norcross, J. C., Geller, J. D., & Kurzawa, E. K. (2000). Conducting psychotherapy with psychotherapists: Prevalence, patients, and problems. *Psychotherapy, 37,* 199–206.

Nouwen, H. J. (1972). *The wounded healer.* Garden City, NY: Doubleday.

O'Connor, M. F. (2001). On the etiology and effective management of professional distress and impairment among psychologists. *Professional Psychology: Research and Practice, 32*(4), 345–350.

O'Connor, M. F. (2000, May). Caring for ourselves [Letter to the editor]. *Monitor of Psychology,* p. 8.

O'Hanlon, W. (1999, July). *Keeping your soul alive: Spiritual, personal, and professional renewal.* Workshop presented at the 16th Annual Cape Cod Summer Symposia, Eastham, MA.

Ornish, D. (1993). *Eat more, weigh less.* New York: Harper Collins.

Orr, P. (1997). Psychology impaired? *Professional Psychology: Research & Practice, 28,* 293–296.

Palumbo, D. (2000, September–October). The burnt-out therapist. *Networker,* pp. 64–69.

Pantano, L. (1997, August). *Achievement awards for helping psychologists take care of themselves.* Paper presented at the Board of Convention Affairs Miniconvention at the 105th annual convention of the American Psychological Association, Chicago.

Pargament, K. I. (1997). *The psychology of religion and coping.* New York: Guilford Press.

Parloff, M. B. (1999, Winter). When should the therapist retire? *Washington School of Psychiatry News,* pp. 3, 6.

Parvin, R., & Anderson, G. (1999). What are we worth? Fee decisions of psychologists in private practice. *Women and Therapy, 22*(3), 15–25.

Pearlman, L. A., & Saakvitne, K. W. (1995). *Trauma and the therapist—Countertransference and vicarious traumatization in psychotherapy with incest survivors.* New York: W. W. Norton.

Pennebaker, J. W. (1990). *Opening up: The healing power of confiding in others.* New York: William Morrow.

Pennebaker, J. W. (1995). *Emotion, disclosure, and health.* Washington, DC: American Psychological Association.

Pennebaker, J. W., Kiecolt-Glaser, J. K., & Glaser, R. (1988). Disclosure of traumas and immune function: Health implications for psychotherapy. *Journal of Consulting and Clinical Psychology, 56,* 239–245.

Perlman, S. D. (1999). *The therapist's emotional survival: Dealing with the pain of exploring trauma.* Northvale, NJ: Jason Aronson.

Peterson, M. (1992). *At personal risk: Boundary violations in professional-client relationships.* New York: W. W. Norton.

Pion, G. M., Mednick, M. T., Astin, H. S., Ljima Hall, C., Kenkel, M. B., Keeta, G. P., et al. (1996). The shifting gender composition of psychology: Trends and implications for the discipline. *American Psychologist, 51,* 509–528.

Pipher, M. (1994). *Reviving Ophelia.* New York: Ballantine Books.

Pope, K. S. (1999). *Solo practice, experiences, strategies, and Dr. Adams's post.* Division 42 Listserv.

Pope, K. S., Sonne, J. L., & Holroyd, J. (1993). *Sexual feelings in psychotherapy: Explorations for therapists and therapists-in-training.* Washington, DC: American Psychological Association.

Pope, K. S., & Tabachnick, B. G. (1993). Therapists' anger, hate, fear, and sexual feelings: National survey of therapist responses, client characteristics, critical events, formal complaints, and training. *Professional Psychology: Research and Practice, 24,* 142–152.

Pope, K. S., & Tabachnick, B. (1994). Therapists as patients: A national survey of psychologists' experiences, problems, and beliefs. *Professional Psychology: Research and Practice, 25,* 247–258.

Pope, K. S., & Vasquez, M. J. T. (1998). *Ethics in psychotherapy and counseling*

(2nd ed.). San Francisco, CA: Jossey-Bass.

Pope, K. S., & Vetter, V. A. (1992). Ethical dilemmas encountered by members of the American Psychological Association. *American Psychologist, 47,* 397–411.

Progoff, I. (1992). *At a journal workshop: The basic text and guide for using the Intensive Journal process.* New York: Dialogue House Library.

Rabasca, L. (1999, March). Help for coping with the stresses of today's practice. *APA Monitor,* p. 23.

Rabinor, J. R. (1995). Overcoming body shame: My client, myself. In M. B. Sussman (Ed.), *A perilous calling: The hazards of psychotherapy practice* (pp. 89–99). New York: John Wiley & Sons.

Rabinor, J. R. (1999). Caring for the caregiver: Healing ourselves. *The Perspective: A Professional Journal of the Renfrew Center Foundation, 5*(1), 1–3.

Rabinor, J. R. (2000). Still becoming a therapist. *The Perspective: Professional Journal of the Renfrew Center Foundation, 6*(1), 13–14.

Rabinor, J. R., & Kearney-Cooke, A. (1998, November). *Rituals for renewal: Caring for caregivers.* Keynote presentation at the Seventh Renfrew Foundation Conference, Philadelphia.

Racusin, G. R., Abramowitz, S. I., & Winter, W. D. (1981). Becoming a therapist: Family dynamics and career choice. *Professional Psychology, 23,* 271–279.

Radeke, J. T., & Mahoney, M. J. (2000). Comparing the personal lives of psychotherapists and research psychologists. *Professional Psychology: Research and Practice, 31,* 82–84.

Rainer, T. (1978). *The new diary: How to use a journal for self-guidance and expanded creativity.* Los Angeles: Jeremy P. Tarcher.

Ratey, J. J. (with Johnson, C.). (1998). *Shadow syndromes.* New York: Bantam Doubleday Dell.

Rehnke, M. A. F. (1997). *Guide to spiritual retreats in the Washington, DC area.* Alexandria, VA: Author.

Rippere, V., & Williams, R. (Eds.). (1985). *Wounded healers: Mental health workers' experiences of depression.* Chichester, England: Wiley.

Riskin, V. (Executive Producer), & Rintels, D. W. (Writer/Producer). (1990). *The*

last best year [Motion picture]. United States: Gideon Productions.

Ryff, C. D., & Singer, B. (1998). The contours of positive human health. *Psychological Inquiry, 9*(1), 1–28.

Saakvitne, K. W., & Pearlman, L. A. (1996). *Transforming the pain: A workbook on vicarious traumatization.* New York: W. W. Norton.

Samuel, S. E., & Gorton, G. E. (1998). National survey of psychology internship directors regarding education for prevention of psychology-patient sexual exploitation. *Professional Psychology: Research and Practice, 29,* 86–90.

Sapienza, B. G. (1997, August). *Keeping our instruments fine tuned: An existential-humanistic perspective.* Paper presented at the 105th annual convention of the American Psychological Association, Chicago.

Sarton, M. (1984). *At seventy—A journal.* New York: W. W. Norton.

Savlin, M. (1995). In the know. *Voices: The Art and Science of Psychotherapy, 3*(2), 3.

Schneider, S. (2001). *A new way to cook.* New York: Artisan.

Schoener, G. R. (1999). Practicing what we preach. *Counseling Psychologist, 27,* 693–701.

Schoener, G. R., & Gonsiorek, J. C. (1988). Assessment and development of rehabilitation plans for counselors who have sexually exploited their clients. *Journal of Counseling and Development, 67,* 227–232.

Schwebel, N., Skorina, J. K., & Schoener, G. (1988). *Assisting impaired psychologists: Program development for state psychological associations.* Washington, DC: American Psychological Association, APA Advisory Committee on Impaired Psychologists, APA Board of Professional Affairs.

Seligman, M. E. P., & Csikszentmihalyi, M. (2000). Positive psychology: An introduction. *American Psychologist, 55,* 5–14.

Shapiro, B. (1997, October). Practitioners must prepare for the worst case scenario. *Monitor on Psychology,* p. 19.

Sheehy, G. (1995). *New passages: Mapping your life across time.* New York: Random House.

Shellenberger, S. (1997). Losing one's match: A proposed model of imago grief therapy. *Journal of Imago Relationship Therapy, 2*(2), 37–54.

Shellenberger, S., & Phelps, G. L. (1997). When it never stops hurting: A case of chronic pain. In S. H. McDaniel (Ed.), *The shared experience of illness: Stories of patients, families and their therapists* (pp. 231–241). New York: Basic Books.

Sherman, M. D., & Thelen, M. H. (1998). Distress and professional impairment among psychologists in clinical practice. *Professional Psychology: Research & Practice, 29,* 79–85.

Shernoff, M. (1995). AIDS: The therapist's journey. In M. B. Sussman (Ed.), *A perilous calling: The hazards of psychotherapy practice* (pp. 139–147). New York: Wiley.

Shuman, D. W., & Foote, W. (1999). Jaffe v. Redmond's impact: After the Supreme Court's recognition of a psychotherapist–patient priviledge. *Professional Psychology: Research and Practice, 30,* 479–487.

Skovholt, T. M. (2001). *The resilient practitioner: Burnout prevention and self-care strategies for counselors, therapists, teachers, and health professionals.* Needham Heights, MA: Allyn & Bacon.

Skovholt, T. M., & Jennings, L. (1999). *Burnout prevention and treatment: Helping the helper.* Phoenix, AZ: Practice Information Clearinghouse of Knowledge.

Skovholt, T. M., & Ronnestad, M. H. (2001). The long, textured path from novice to senior practitioner. In T. M. Skovholt (Ed.), *The resilient practitioner: Burnout prevention and self-care strategies for counselors, therapists, teachers, and health professionals* (pp. 25–54). Needham Heights, MA: Allyn & Bacon.

Slakter, E. (Ed.). (1987). *Countertransference.* Northvale, NJ: Jason Aronson.

Smyth, J. M., & Greenberg, M. A. (2000). Scriptotherapy: The effects of writing about traumatic events. In P. R. Duberstein & J. M. Masling (Eds.), *Psychodynamic perspectives on sickness and health* (pp. 121–163). Washington, DC: American Psychological Association.

Smyth, J. M., & Pennebaker, J. W. (1999). Sharing one's story: Translating emotional experiences into words as a coping tool. In C. R. Snyder (Ed.), *Coping: The psychology of what works* (pp. 70–89). New York: Oxford University Press.

Smyth, J. M., Stone, A. A., Hurewitz, A., & Kaell, A. (1999). Effects of writing about stressful experiences on symptom reduction in patients with asthma or rheumatoid arthritis: A randomized trial. *Journal of the American Medical Association, 281,* 1304–1309.

Solzhenitsyn, A. I. (1968). *The first circle.* New York: Harper & Row.

Stamm, B. H. (Ed.). (1995). *Secondary traumatic stress: Self-care issues for clinicians, researchers, and educators.* Lutherville, MD: Sidran Press.

Starr, B., & Weiner, M. B. (2000). *Niche practice speciality: Guidelines for spirituality and psychotherapy.* Unpublished manuscript.

St. Clair, M. (1986). *Object relations and self psychology.* Monterey, CA: Brooks/Cole.

Strauss, H. (1996). Working as an elder analyst. In B. Gerson (Ed.), *The therapist as a person: Life crises, life choices, life experiences, and their effects on treatment* (pp. 277–294). Hillsdale, NJ: Analytic Press.

Strupp, H. H. (1996). The tripartite model and the *Consumer Reports* study. *American Psychologist, 51,* 1017–1024.

Surrey, J. L. (1985). *The "self-in-relation": A theory of women's development* (Working Paper 13). Wellesley, MA: Stone Center.

Sussman, M. B. (1992). *A curious calling: Unconscious motivations for practicing psychotherapy.* Northvale, NJ: Jason Aronson.

Sussman, M. B. (1995). *A perilous calling: The hazards of psychotherapy practice.* New York: Wiley.

Tallmadge, K. (2002). *Diet simple.* Washington, DC: Lifeline Press.

Thoreson, R. W., & Skorina, J. K. (1986). Alcohol abuse among psychologists. In R. R. Kilburg, P. E. Nathan, & R. W. Thoreson (Eds.), *Professionals in distress: Issues, syndromes, and solutions in psychology* (pp. 77–117). Washington, DC: American Psychological Association.

Titelman, P. (Ed.). (1987). *The therapist's own family.* Northvale, NJ: Jason Aronson.

Treadway, D. (1998, January–February). Riding out the storm. *The Networker,* pp. 54–61.

Ukens, C. (1995, November 6). The tragic truth. *Drug Topics, 139*(21), 66.

U.S. Department of Health and Human Services. (2000). Mental health, United States, 2000. Retrieved June 1, 2002, from http://www.mentalhealth.org/ publications / allpubs / SMA01-3537 / default.asp

van der Kolk, B. A., McFarlane, A. C., & Weisaeth, L. (Eds). (1996). *Traumatic stress: The effects of overwhelming experience on mind, body, and society.* New York: Guilford Press.

Vaughan, S. (1998) *The talking cure: The science behind the psychotherapy.* New York: Henry Holt.

Wachs, T. D. (2000). *Necessary but not sufficient: The respective roles of single and multiple influences of individual development.* Washington, DC: American Psychological Association.

Welch, B. W. (1998). Walking the documentation tightrope. In *Insight: Safeguarding psychologists against liability risks I.* Amityville, NY: American Professional Agency.

Welch, B. W. (1999). Boundary violations: In the eye of the beholder. In *Insight: Safeguarding psychologists against liability risks I.* Amityville, NY: American Professional Agency.

Welt, S. R., & Herron, W. G. (1990). *Narcissism and the psychotherapist.* New York: Guilford Press.

Wepman, B. (1997). Fathers and sons: Introduction. *Voices: The Art and Science of Psychotherapy, 33*(4), 39–41.

Winnicott, D. W. (1965). *The Maturational Processes and the faciliatory environment: Studies in the theory of emotional development.* New York: International Universities Press.

Wittine, B. (1995). The spiritual self: Its relevance in the development and daily life of the psychotherapist. In M. B. Sussman (Ed.), *A perilous calling: The hazards of psychotherapy practice* (pp. 288–301). New York: Wiley.

Yalom, I. D. (1989). *Love's executioner and other tales of psychotherapy.* New York: Basic Books.

Yutrzenka, B. A. (1995). Making a case for training in ethnic and cultural diversity in increasing treatment efficacy. *Journal of Consulting and Clinical Psychology, 63,* 197–206.

Zager, D. (1988). Women, private practice and the family: Special needs/special problems. *Psychology in Private Practice, 6,* 9–14.

Ziegler, J. L., & Kanas, N. (1986). Coping with stress during internship. In C. D. Scott & J. Hawk (Eds.), *Heal thyself: The health of health care professionals* (pp. 174–184). New York: Brunner/Mazel.

Author Index

Subject Index

About the Author

Ellen Baker, PhD, is a psychologist in private practice in Washington, DC. Previously, she was on staff at the Veterans Administration Medical Centers of Washington, DC, and Palo Alto, California, and the Washington Women's Medical Center. Dr. Baker has trained in psychodrama at St. Elizabeth's Hospital in Washington, DC. She is the coeditor of *Experimental Therapies for Eating Disorders* (1989) with Lynne M. Hornyak. She has served in the governance of the District of Columbia Psychological Association and the Division of Independent Practice of the American Psychological Association (APA; division 42).

For over 15 years, Dr. Baker has written, consulted, and led experiential workshops on therapist well-being. She has a particular interest in personal journal writing as a means of therapist self care, and as an expressive art form. Dr. Baker also serves as an APA media contact, providing interviews for numerous broadcast and print venues around the country on the therapeutic benefits of personal journal writing. She also hosted a series of workshops at the National Museum of Women in the Arts in Washington, DC, on journal writing as a folk art form.

Dr. Baker received her PhD from the University of Wisconsin-Madison in 1976.